LEISURE ARTS
the art of everyday living
www.leisurearts.com

MW00388642

Best of

Baby & Kids Quilts

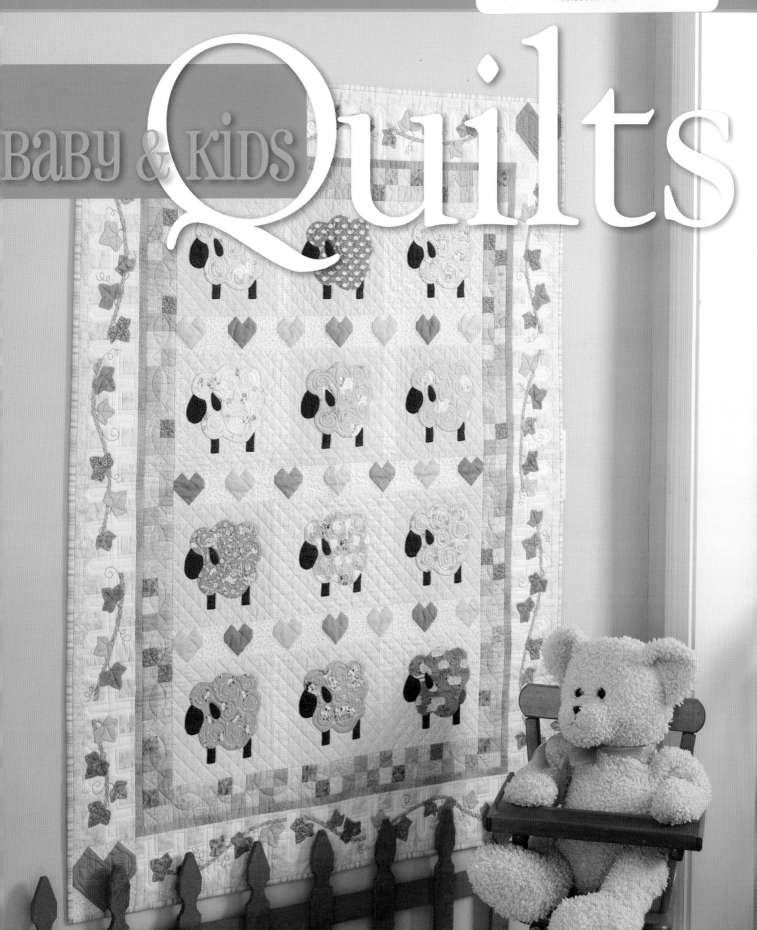

FONS & PORTER STAFF
Editors-in-Chief Marianne Fons and Liz Porter

Editor Jean Nolte
Assistant Editor Diane Tomlinson
Managing Editor Debra Finan
Technical Writer Kristine Peterson

Art Director Tony Jacobson

Editorial Assistant Cinde Alexander
Sewing Specialist Cindy Hathaway

Contributing Photographers Craig Anderson, Dean Tanner, Katie Downey
Contributing Photo Assistant DeElda Wittmack

Publisher Kristi Loeffelholz
Advertising Manager Cristy Adamski
Retail Manager Sharon Hart
Web Site Manager Phillip Zacharias
Customer Service Manager Tiffiny Bond
Fons & Porter Staff Peggy Garner, Shelle Goodwin, Allison McNeal, Kimberly Romero, Laura Saner, Karol Skeffington, Yvonne Smith, Natalie Wakeman, Anne Welker, Karla Wesselmann

New Track Media LLC
President and CEO Stephen J. Kent
Chief Financial Officer Mark F. Arnett
President, Book Publishing W. Budge Wallis
Vice President/Publishing Director Joel P. Toner
Vice President, Circulation Nicole McGuire
Vice President, Production Barbara Schmitz
Production Manager Dominic M. Taormina
IT Manager Denise Donnarumma
New Business Manager Susan Sidler
Renewal and Billing Manager Nekeya Dancy
Online Subscriptions Manager Jodi Lee

Our Mission Statement
Our goal is for you to enjoy making quilts as much as we do.

LEISURE ARTS STAFF
Editor-in-Chief Susan White Sullivan
Quilt and Craft Publications Director Cheryl Johnson
Special Projects Director Susan Frantz Wiles
Senior Prepress Director Mark Hawkins
Imaging Technician Stephanie Johnson
Prepress Technician Janie Marie Wright
Publishing Systems Administrator Becky Riddle
Mac Information Technology Specialist Robert Young

President and Chief Executive Officer Rick Barton
Vice President and Chief Operations Officer Tom Siebenmorgen
Vice President of Sales Mike Behar
Director of Finance and Administration Laticia Mull Dittrich
National Sales Director Martha Adams
Creative Services Chaska Lucas
Information Technology Director Hermine Linz
Controller Francis Caple
Vice President, Operations Jim Dittrich
Retail Customer Service Manager Stan Raynor
Print Production Manager Fred F. Pruss

Library of Congress Control Number: 2011930609
ISBN-13/EAN: 978-1-60900-249-7
10 9 8 7 6 5 4 3 2 1

We're thrilled to bring you this
collection of some of our very favorite
quilts for the young people in your life!
The projects we've included are among
our most popular of all time. You'll
find patchwork for all skill levels, plus
dashes of lovely appliqué. Enjoy the
beautiful photography as you browse through the pages to find the quilt that's
just right for you. Whether you want to make a quilt for a baby, toddler, or teen,
you'll find plenty to love. You'll also appreciate our trademarked *Sew Easy*
lessons that will guide you via step-by-step photography through any project-
specific special techniques. We think you'll have fun stitching these quilts for
the babies and kids you know!

Happy quilting,

Marianne & Liz

Techniques

54

90

120

Celebrate a New Star

Designer Cheryl Malkowski made this baby announcement quilt to celebrate the arrival of her first grandchild. Personalize your quilt to welcome a little one.

PROJECT RATING: INTERMEDIATE

Size: 40" × 52"

Blocks: 1 (12") Star block

MATERIALS

10 fat quarters★ assorted medium and dark yellow, green, blue, purple, and pink prints

2 yards white print

2½ yards backing fabric

Crib-size quilt batting

★fat quarter = 18" × 20"

NOTE: Fabrics in the quilt shown are from the Spellbound collection by P&B Textiles.

Cutting

Measurements include ¼" seam allowances. Border strips are exact length needed. You may want to make them longer to allow for piecing variations.

NOTE: To make photo block, refer to *Sew Easy: Printing on Fabric* on page 11. Trim printed photo to 4½" square.

From white print, cut:

• 1 (12½"-wide) strip. From strip, cut 1 (12½" × 13½") H rectangle.

NOTE: If desired, print baby's name, birth date, height, and weight on H rectangle, as shown in photo on page 10. Refer to *Sew Easy: Printing on Fabric* on page 11.

• 2 (5¼"-wide) strips. From strips, cut 11 (5¼") squares. Cut squares in half diagonally in both directions to make 44 quarter-square A triangles (2 are extra).

• 3 (4½"-wide) strips. From strips, cut 1 (4½" × 32½") D rectangle, 1 (4½" × 28½") G rectangle, and 7 (4½") C squares.

- 6 (3½"-wide) strips. From 1 strip, cut 1 (3½" × 28½") F rectangle. Piece remaining strips to make 2 (3½" × 40½") top and bottom outer borders and 2 (3½" × 46½") side outer borders.
- 2 (2½"-wide) strips. From strips, cut 1 (2½" × 16½") J rectangle and 2 (2½" × 12½") I rectangles.
- 2 (1½"-wide) strips. From strips, cut 1 (1½" × 32½") E rectangle and 1 (1½" × 16½") K rectangle.

From medium yellow print, cut:
- 2 (4⅞"-wide) strips. From strips, cut 4 (4⅞") squares. Cut squares in half diagonally to make 8 half-square B triangles.
- 1 (2¼"-wide) strip for binding.
- 1 (1½"-wide) strip for inner border.

From dark yellow print, cut:
- 1 (5¼"-wide) strip. From strip, cut 2 (5¼") squares. Cut squares in half diagonally in both directions to make 8 quarter-square A triangles.
- 1 (2¼"-wide) strip for binding.
- 1 (1½"-wide) strip for inner border.

From medium green print, cut:
- 1 (5¼"-wide) strip. From strip, cut 1 (5¼") square and 1 (4⅞") square. Cut 5¼" square in half diagonally in both directions to make 4 quarter-square A triangles. Cut 4⅞" square in half diagonally to make 2 half-square B triangles.
- 1 (4⅞"-wide) strip. From strip, cut 3 (4⅞") squares. Cut squares in half diagonally to make 6 half-square B triangles (1 is extra).
- 1 (2¼"-wide) strip for binding.
- 1 (1½"-wide) strip for inner border.

From dark green print, cut:
- 1 (5¼"-wide) strip. From strip, cut 2 (5¼") squares. Cut squares in half diagonally in both directions to make 8 quarter-square A triangles (1 is extra).

- 1 (2¼"-wide) strip for binding.
- 1 (1½"-wide) strip for inner border.

From medium blue print, cut:
- 2 (4⅞"-wide) strips. From strips, cut 5 (4⅞") squares. Cut squares in half diagonally to make 10 half-square B triangles.
- 1 (2¼"-wide) strip for binding.
- 1 (1½"-wide) strip for inner border.

From dark blue print, cut:
- 1 (5¼"-wide) strip. From strip, cut 3 (5¼") squares. Cut squares in half diagonally in both directions to make 12 quarter-square A triangles (2 are extra).
- 1 (4⅞"-wide) strip. From strip, cut 2 (4⅞") squares. Cut squares in half diagonally to make 4 half-square B triangles.
- 1 (2¼"-wide) strip for binding.
- 1 (1½"-wide) strip for inner border.

From medium purple print, cut:
- 2 (4⅞"-wide) strips. From strips, cut 4 (4⅞") squares. Cut squares in half diagonally to make 8 half-square B triangles (1 is extra).
- 1 (2¼"-wide) strip for binding.
- 1 (1½"-wide) strip for inner border.

From dark purple print, cut:
- 1 (5¼"-wide) strip. From strip, cut 2 (5¼") squares. Cut squares in half diagonally in both directions to make 8 quarter-square A triangles (1 is extra).
- 1 (2¼"-wide) strip for binding.
- 1 (1½"-wide) strip for inner border.

From medium pink print, cut:
- 1 (4⅞"-wide) strip. From strip, cut 3 (4⅞") squares. Cut squares in half diagonally to make 6 half-square B triangles.
- 1 (2¼"-wide) strip for binding.
- 1 (1½"-wide) strip for inner border.

From dark pink print, cut:
- 1 (5¼"-wide) strip. From strip, cut 2 (5¼") squares. Cut squares in half diagonally in both directions to make 8 quarter-square A triangles (2 are extra).
- 1 (2¼"-wide) strip for binding.
- 1 (1½"-wide) strip for inner border.

Ribbon Row Assembly

1. Join 1 medium yellow print B triangle, 1 dark yellow print A triangle, and 1 white print A triangle as shown in *Ribbon Unit Diagrams*. Make 8 yellow ribbon units.

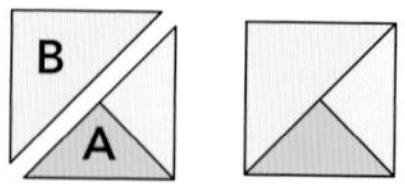

Ribbon Unit Diagrams

2. In the same manner, using medium print B triangles, dark print A triangles, and white print A triangles, make 7 green ribbon units, 10 blue ribbon units, 7 purple ribbon units, and 6 pink ribbon units.

3. Join yellow ribbon units as shown in *Quilt Top Assembly Diagram* to make yellow ribbon row.

4. In the same manner, join green ribbon units and 1 white print C square to make green ribbon row.

5. Make blue, purple, and pink ribbon rows as shown in *Quilt Top Assembly Diagram*.

Star Block Assembly

1. Make 4 blue/green ribbon units using 1 dark blue print B triangle, 1 medium green print A triangle, and white print A triangle in each.

2. Lay out dark blue/green ribbon units, 4 white print C squares, and 1 photo square as shown in *Block Assembly Diagram*. Join into rows; join rows to complete Star block *(Block Diagram)*.

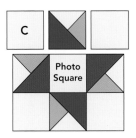

Block Assembly Diagram

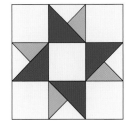

Block Diagram

3. Referring to *Quilt Top Assembly Diagram*, add I rectangles to top and bottom of star block. Add J and K rectangles to sides of block.

Quilt Assembly

1. Lay out ribbon rows, bordered star block, and white print rectangles as shown in *Quilt Top Assembly Diagram*. Join pieces into sections; join sections to complete quilt center.

2. Join assorted 1½"-wide print strips with diagonal seams to make one continuous strip. From strip, cut 2 (1½" × 44½") side inner borders and 2 (1½" × 34½") top and bottom inner borders.

3. Add side inner borders to quilt center. Add top and bottom inner borders to quilt.

4. Repeat for white print outer borders.

Finishing

1. Divide backing fabric into 2 (1¼-yard) lengths. Cut 1 piece in half lengthwise to make 2 narrow panels. Join 1 narrow panel to wider panel. Seam will run

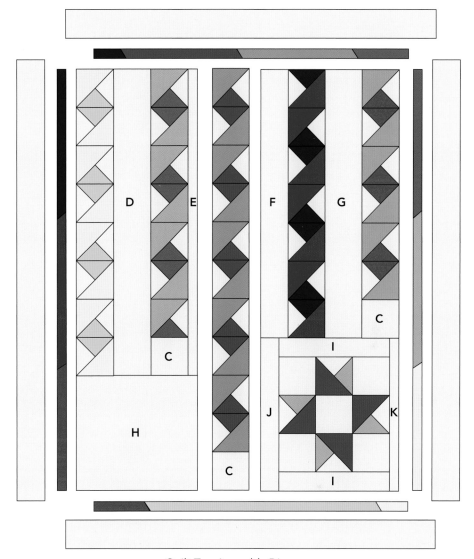

Quilt Top Assembly Diagram

horizontally. Remaining panel is extra and can be used to make a hanging sleeve.

2. Layer backing, batting, and quilt top; baste. Quilt as desired. Quilt shown was quilted with an overall design using variegated thread *(Quilting Diagram)*.

3. Join 2¼"-wide assorted print strips into 1 continuous piece for straight-grain French-fold binding. Add binding to quilt.

Quilting Diagram

Jack Reichelt
July 11, 2007
7 lbs, 20 1/2"

DESIGNER

Author and teacher Cheryl Malkowski loves everything about quilting, as long as it can be done by machine. Look for her latest book, *Blocks to Diamonds: Kaleidoscope Star Quilts from Traditional Blocks,* published by C&T.

Contact her at:

www.cherylrosecreations.com

Sew Easy™
Printing on Fabric

Bring a quilt to life with your favorite family photos.
Use an inkjet printer to personalize your next project.

1. Prepare image for printing on your computer. Use a digital photo, scan a photo or other image, or create a design using a software program.

2. Trim any loose threads from edges of fabric sheet—do not pull them. If fabric sheet is curled, use a hot iron on the paper side or weight it down overnight with books.

3. Adjust printer settings to plain paper (or thick paper if printer has this option) and best quality. **Use an inkjet printer only.** Test your printout on paper to check image clarity, size, and placement before printing on fabric sheet.

4. Load fabric sheet in printer tray so image will print on fabric side. Follow your printer's directions for loading instructions. (Fabric sheets may feed best if loaded one at a time.)

5. Print image. Allow ink to dry completely (about 15 minutes).

6. Peel paper backing from fabric sheet.

7. To remove excess ink, soak fabric sheet in room temperature water for 10 minutes, then gently rinse.

8. Lay flat to dry. Do not twist or wring fabric to remove excess water. When fabric is completely dry, iron, using lowest steam setting to remove any wrinkles.

NOTE: To prevent fading, do not place printed image in direct sunlight.

TRIED & TRUE

Make a 24" square table topper.

MATERIALS

2 fat quarters★ dark and light brown prints
2 fat eighths★★ medium brown and blue prints
½ yard cream print
★fat quarter = 18" × 20"
★★fat eighth = 9" × 20"

Cutting

From dark brown print, cut:
• 4 (5¼") squares. Cut squares in half diagonally in both directions to make 16 quarter-square A triangles.
• 2 (4⅞") squares. Cut squares in half diagonally to make 4 half-square B triangles.

From light brown print, cut:
• 8 (4⅞") squares. Cut squares in half diagonally to make 16 half-square B triangles.

From medium brown print, cut:
• 1 (5¼") square. Cut square in half diagonally in both directions to make 4 quarter-square A triangles.
• 1 (4½") C square.

From blue print, cut:
• 2 (4⅞") squares. Cut squares in half diagonally to make 4 half-square B triangles.

From cream print, cut:
• 5 (5¼") squares. Cut squares in half diagonally in both directions to make 20 quarter-square A triangles.
• 2 (4⅞") squares. Cut squares in half diagonally to make 4 half-square B triangles.
• 4 (4½") C squares.
• 2 (2½" × 16½") strips.
• 2 (2½" × 12½") strips. ✳

Make this cheerful baby quilt with bright pinwheels and smiling flowers.

Happy Flowers

PROJECT RATING: EASY
Size: 35" × 35"
Blocks: 5 (9") Pinwheel blocks
4 (9") Flower blocks

MATERIALS

5 fat eighths★ assorted bright prints in teal, yellow, blue, red, and orange for blocks

4 fat eighths★ assorted bright solids in blue, green, red, and orange for blocks and sashing squares

1 fat eighth★ yellow print for Flower Centers

¾ yard white print

⅜ yard light blue print

⅜ yard dark blue print

⅜ yard multi-color print for binding

Paper-backed fusible web

1¼ yards backing fabric

Crib-size quilt batting

Black and red embroidery floss

★fat eighth = 9" × 20"

Cutting

Patterns for appliqué shapes are on page 17. Follow manufacturer's instructions for using fusible web. Measurements include ¼" seam allowances.

From each bright print fat eighth, cut:

• 1 (5⅜"-wide) strip. From strip, cut 2 (5⅜") squares. Cut squares in half diagonally to make 4 half-square B triangles.

From each of 4 bright print fat eighths, cut:

• 5 Outer Petals.

From each bright solid fat eighth, cut:

• 1 (2½"-wide) strip. From strip, cut 4 (2½") sashing squares.

• 5 Inner Petals.

From yellow print fat eighth, cut:

• 4 Flower Centers.

From white print, cut:

• 1 (9½"-wide) strip. From strip, cut 4 (9½") A squares.

• 2 (5⅜"-wide) strips. From strips, cut 10 (5⅜") squares. Cut squares in half diagonally to make 20 half-square B triangles.

From light blue print, cut:

• 3 (2½"-wide) strips. From strips, cut 12 (2½" × 9½") sashing strips.

From dark blue print, cut:

• 3 (2½"-wide) strips. From strips, cut 12 (2½" × 9½") sashing strips.

From multi-color print, cut:

• 4 (2¼"-wide) strips for binding.

Flower Block Assembly

1. Referring to *Flower Block Diagram*, arrange 5 matching Outer Petals, 5 matching Inner Petals, and 1 Flower Center on white print A square. Fuse pieces in place.

Flower Block Diagram

2. Using matching thread, machine blanket stitch around appliqué pieces.

3. Referring to Flower Center pattern and *Stitch Diagrams*, satin stitch eyes on flower center using 2 strands of black embroidery floss. Satin stitch hearts using 2 strands of red embroidery floss. Stem stitch mouth using 2 strands of red embroidery floss. Make 4 Flower Blocks.

Stem Stitch

Satin Stitch

Stitch Diagrams

Pinwheel Block Assembly

1. Choose 4 matching bright print B triangles and 4 white print B triangles. Join 1 bright print triangle and 1 white print triangle as shown in *Triangle-Square Diagrams.* Make 4 triangle-squares.

Triangle-Square Diagrams

2. Lay out triangle-squares as shown in *Pinwheel Block Assembly Diagram.* Join into rows; join rows to make 1 Pinwheel block *(Pinwheel Block Diagram).* Make 5 Pinwheel blocks.

Pinwheel Block Assembly Diagram

Pinwheel Block Diagram

Quilt Assembly

1. Lay out Flower blocks, Pinwheel blocks, sashing strips, and sashing squares as shown in *Quilt Top Assembly Diagram.*

2. Join into rows; join rows to complete quilt top.

Finishing

1. Layer backing, batting, and quilt top; baste. Quilt as desired. Quilt shown was quilted in the ditch, with echo quilting ¼" around the flowers, and with a wavy line inside each Flower block *(Quilting Diagram).*

Quilt Top Assembly Diagram

2. Join 2¼"-wide multi-color print strips into 1 continuous piece for straight-grain French-fold binding. Add binding to quilt.

Quilting Diagram

TRIED & TRUE

Bright checks, dots, and stripes from Pop Parade by
Metro for P&B Textiles make this a lively table topper.

SIZE OPTIONS

	Table Topper (13" × 35")	Throw (57" × 79")
Blocks	2 (9") Flower blocks	17 (9") Flower blocks
	1 (9") Pinwheel block	18 (9") Pinwheel blocks

MATERIALS

Assorted Bright Prints	1 fat eighth★	9 fat quarters★★
Assorted Bright Solids	2 fat eighths★	9 fat quarters★★
Yellow Print	1 fat eighth★	1 fat quarter★★
White Print	1 fat quarter★★	2½ yards
Light Blue Print	1 fat eighth★	1¼ yards
Dark Blue Print	¼ yard	½ yard
Multi-color Print	¼ yard	⅝ yard
Backing Fabric	½ yard	4¾ yards
Batting	Crib-size	Twin-size

★★fat quarter = 18" × 20"

★fat eighth = 9" × 20"

**WEB** EXTRA

Go to FonsandPorter.com/happysizes to download *Quilt Top Assembly Diagrams* for these size options.

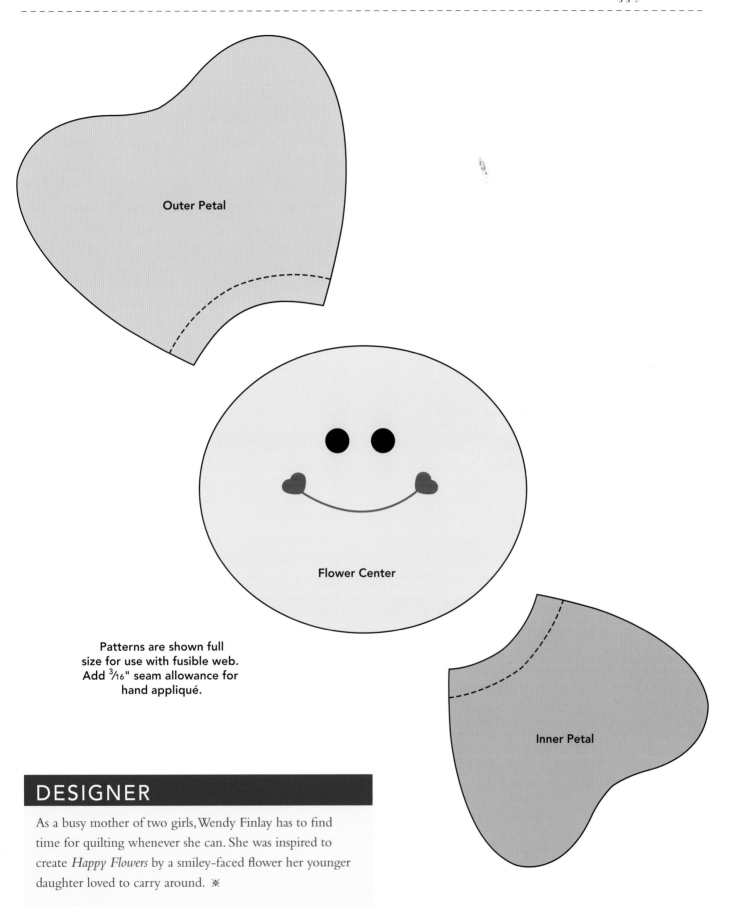

Outer Petal

Flower Center

Patterns are shown full
size for use with fusible web.
Add ³⁄₁₆" seam allowance for
hand appliqué.

Inner Petal

DESIGNER

As a busy mother of two girls, Wendy Finlay has to find
time for quilting whenever she can. She was inspired to
create *Happy Flowers* by a smiley-faced flower her younger
daughter loved to carry around. ❋

Baby's Star

This graphic quilt is sure to get baby's attention!
It's so quick and easy, you can piece it in an afternoon.

PROJECT RATING: EASY
Size: 48" × 48"

MATERIALS

½ yard red print
½ yard green print
⅜ yard blue print
⅜ yard black print
⅜ yard white print
1½ yards yellow print
3 yards backing fabric
Twin-size quilt batting

Cutting

Measurements include ¼" seam allowances. Border strips are exact length needed. You may want to make them longer to allow for piecing variations.

From red print, cut:

- 3 (4⅞"-wide) strips. From strips, cut 18 (4⅞") squares. Cut squares in half diagonally to make 36 half-square triangles.

From green print, cut:

- 3 (4⅞"-wide) strips. From strips, cut 18 (4⅞") squares. Cut squares in half diagonally to make 36 half-square triangles.

From blue print, cut:

- 4 (2½"-wide) strips. From strips, cut 2 (2½" × 28½") top and bottom inner borders and 2 (2½" × 24½") side inner borders.

From black print, cut:

- 4 (2½"-wide) strips for strip sets.

From white print, cut:

- 4 (2½"-wide) strips for strip sets.

From yellow print, cut:

- 5 (6½"-wide) strips. From strips, cut 2 (6½" × 36½") side outer borders. Piece remaining strips to make 2 (6½" × 48½") top and bottom outer borders.
- 6 (2¼"-wide) strips for binding.

Center Assembly

1. Join 1 red print half-square triangle and 1 green print half-square triangle as shown in *Triangle-Square Diagrams*. Make 36 triangle-squares.

Triangle-Square Diagrams

2. Lay out triangle-squares as shown in *Quilt Top Assembly Diagram*. Join into horizontal rows; join rows to complete quilt center.

Quilt Assembly

1. Add blue print side inner borders to quilt center. Add blue print top and bottom inner borders to quilt.

2. Join 1 black print strip and 1 white print strip as shown in *Strip Set Diagram*. Make 4 strip sets. From strip sets, cut 64 (2½"-wide) segments.

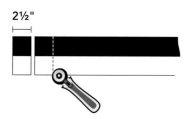

Strip Set Diagram

3. Referring to *Quilt Top Assembly Diagram*, join 14 segments to make 1 side middle border. Make 2 side middle borders. In the same manner, join 18 segments to make top middle border. Repeat for bottom middle border.

4. Add side middle borders to quilt center. Add top and bottom middle borders to quilt.

5. Add yellow print side outer borders to quilt center. Add top and bottom outer borders to quilt.

Finishing

1. Divide backing into 2 (1½-yard) lengths. Cut 1 piece in half lengthwise to make 2 narrow panels. Join 1 narrow panel to wider panel. Remaining panel is extra and can be used to make a hanging sleeve.

2. Layer backing, batting, and quilt top; baste. Quilt as desired. Quilt shown was quilted with an allover design of loops and stars *(Quilting Diagram)*.

3. Join (2¼"-wide) yellow print strips into 1 continuous piece for straight-grain French-fold binding. Add binding to quilt.

Quilting Diagram

TRIED & TRUE

Our version, in earthy hues, uses fabrics from the Remember Me collection by Lydia Quigley for Clothworks.

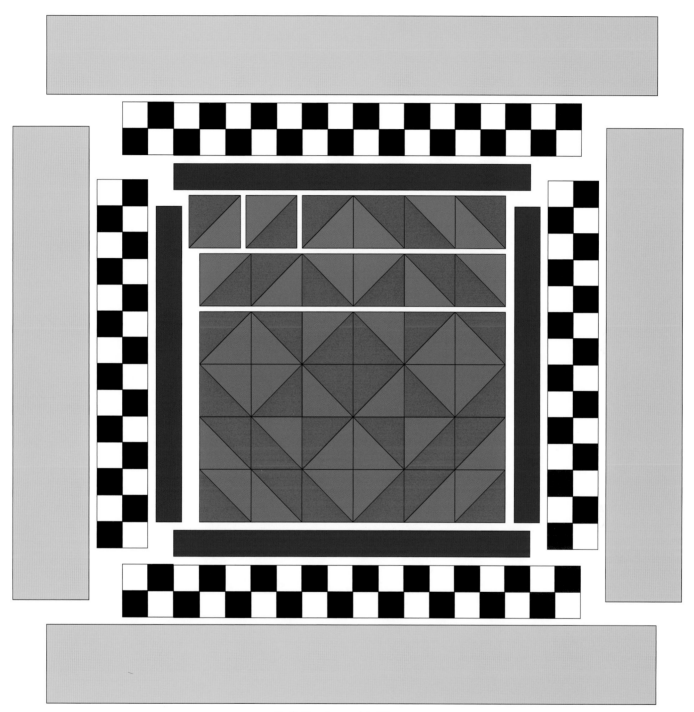

Quilt Top Assembly Diagram

DESIGNER

Angela Brichacek sews or quilts something every day. She is a longarm quilter who loves watching quilting on TV and reading about it in magazines and on the internet.

Contact her at:

redleafquilting@hotmail.com ✳

Baby Craze

This soft and snuggly flannel quilt is perfect for babies and toddlers. It's easy and quick—even the binding is done by machine.

PROJECT RATING: EASY
Size: 42" × 42"
Blocks: 49 (6") Crazy blocks

MATERIALS

17 fat quarters★ assorted flannel prints
1¾ yards muslin
2¾ yards blue flannel for backing and self binding
Crib-size quilt batting
★fat quarter = 18" × 20"

Cutting

Measurements include ¼" seam allowances.

From each flannel fat quarter, cut:
- 1 (3"–4"-wide) strip. From strip, cut 3 (3"–4") squares.
- 2 (6"-wide) strips. From strips, cut 6 (6") squares. Cut squares in half diagonally to make 12 corner triangles.

From muslin, cut:
- 9 (6½"-wide) strips. From strips, cut 49 (6½") squares.

Block Assembly

1. Referring to *Block Assembly Diagrams* on page 24, center 1 flannel square right side up atop 1 muslin square. Place a corner triangle atop center square, right sides facing. Align edges; stitch through all layers.
2. Open triangle and press toward corner. Add a corner triangle to opposite side of center square.
3. Repeat for remaining corners.

Block Assembly Diagrams

4. Trim excess flannel fabric even with edges of muslin square. Using decorative machine stitches and assorted colors of thread, stitch over each seam to complete 1 block *(Block Diagram)*. Make 49 blocks.

Block Diagram

Sew **Smart**™
Position center squares in slightly different positions to vary the look of your blocks. —Marianne

Quilt Assembly

1. Lay out blocks as shown in *Quilt Top Assembly Diagram*.

2. Join into rows; join rows to complete quilt top.

Finishing

1. Divide backing into 2 (1⅜-yard) lengths. Cut 1 piece in half lengthwise to make 2 narrow panels. Join 1 narrow panel to wider panel. Remaining panel is extra and can be used to make a hanging sleeve.

2. Layer backing, batting, and quilt top; baste.

3. Using a decorative stitch and blue thread, quilt along seams between blocks.

Quilt Top Assembly Diagram

4. Trim batting even with edge of quilt top. Trim backing 1" beyond edge of quilt top. Fold backing corner in to meet corner of quilt top *(Corner Diagram)*. Fold raw edges of backing to meet edge of quilt top. Fold backing again, overlapping edge of quilt ½" and forming mitered corner *(Miter Diagram)*. Using machine blanket stitch, stitch edge of binding to quilt. Whipstitch miters closed.

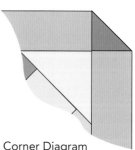

Corner Diagram

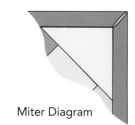

Miter Diagram

SIZE OPTIONS

	Throw (66" × 78")	Twin (66" × 96")
Blocks	143 (6") blocks	176 (6") blocks
Setting	11 × 13	11 × 16

MATERIALS

Assorted Prints	48 fat quarters	59 fat quarters
Muslin	4½ yards	5½ yards
Backing and self binding fabric	4¾ yards	5¾ yards
Batting	Twin-size	Queen-size

Throw Size

Twin Size

DESIGNER

Inspired by her mother-in-law's Aunt Julie, who made quilts for new babies born into the family, Terry Starke continues the tradition. She modeled *Baby Craze* after one of Julie's quilts, which her own three children have used and now her grandson sleeps under when he spends the night. ✳

Baby Strips

A bundle of coordinating fat quarters is the perfect inspiration for this pretty baby quilt.

PROJECT RATING: EASY
Size: 40" × 40"
Blocks: 4 (17¾") blocks

MATERIALS

8 fat quarters★ coordinating prints in pink, yellow, and green
¾ yard yellow print for outer border and binding
2½ yards backing fabric
Crib-size quilt batting
★fat quarter = 18" × 20"

Cutting

Measurements include ¼" seam allowances. Border strips are exact length needed. You may want to make them longer to allow for piecing variations.

From each fat quarter, cut:
• 6 (2"-wide) strips for strip sets.

From remainders of each of 4 prints, cut:
• 2 (1¼"-wide) strips. From strips, cut 4 (1¼" × 9") rectangles for sashing.

From remainder of 1 green print, cut:
• 4 (2") corner squares.

From remainder of 1 pink print, cut:
• 4 (1¼") sashing squares.

From remainders of prints, cut:
• (1¼"-wide) strips of various lengths. Piece strips to make 2 (1¼" × 37½") top and bottom inner borders and 2 (1¼" × 36") side inner borders.

From yellow print, cut:
• 5 (2¼"-wide) strips for binding.
• 4 (2"-wide) strips. From strips, cut 4 (2" × 37½") border strips.

Block Assembly

1. Join 6 assorted (2"-wide) strips as shown in *Strip Set Diagram.* Make 8 strip sets.

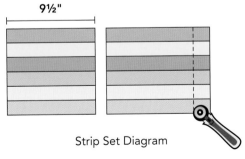

Strip Set Diagram

2. From strip sets, cut 16 (9½") segments. Cut 8 squares in half diagonally from upper left to lower

right corner. Cut remaining squares in half diagonally from lower left to upper right corner *(Cutting Diagrams).* You will have 16 sets of mirror-image triangles.

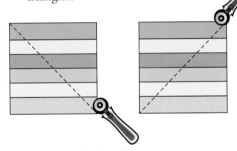

Cutting Diagrams

3. Join 2 mirror-image triangles as shown in *Block Unit Diagrams.* Trim Block Unit to 9" square. Make 16 Block Units.

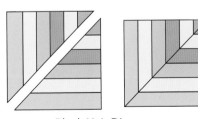

Block Unit Diagrams

4. Referring to *Block Assembly Diagram* on page 28, lay out 4 Block Units, 4 matching sashing rectangles, and 1 sashing square. Join into rows; join rows to complete 1 block *(Block Diagram)*. Make 4 blocks.

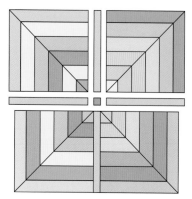

Block Assembly Diagram

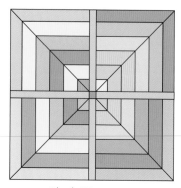

Block Diagram

Quilt Assembly

1. Lay out blocks as shown in *Quilt Top Assembly Diagram*. Join into rows; join rows to complete quilt center.
2. Add pieced side inner borders to quilt center. Add pieced top and bottom inner borders to quilt.
3. Add yellow print side outer borders to quilt center. Join 1 green print corner square to each end of remaining outer borders. Add borders to top and bottom of quilt.

Finishing

1. Divide backing into 2 (1¼-yard) lengths. Cut 1 piece in half lengthwise to make 2 narrow panels. Join 1 narrow panel to wider panel.

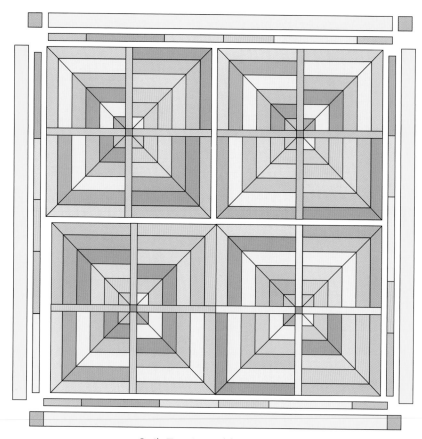

Quilt Top Assembly Diagram

Remaining panel is extra and can be used to make a hanging sleeve.
2. Layer backing, batting, and quilt top; baste. Quilt as desired. Quilt shown was quilted with an allover feather design *(Quilting Diagram)*.
3. Join 2¼"-wide yellow print strips into 1 continuous piece for straight-grain French-fold binding. Add binding to quilt.

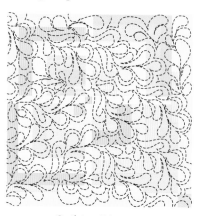

Quilting Diagram

TRIED & TRUE

We used bold prints from the Mulberry collection by Sue Zipkin for Clothworks to make this fun block.

SIZE OPTIONS

	Throw (75½" × 75½")	Twin (75½" × 93¼")	Full (93¼" × 93¼")
Blocks	16	20	25
Setting	4 × 4	4 × 5	5 × 5

MATERIALS

Assorted Prints	32 fat quarters	40 fat quarters	50 fat quarters
Yellow Print	1⅛ yards	1¼ yards	1⅜ yards
Backing Fabric	4½ yards	5½ yards	8¼ yards
Batting	Full-size	Full-size	King-size

Throw Size

Twin Size

Full Size

DESIGNER

Charlotte Gurwell was encouraged to sew by her grandmother, a proficient hand quilter. Charlotte began sewing clothing when she was twelve years old, but didn't make quilts until many years later. She now operates a longarm quilting business in her Jefferson City, Missouri home.

Black & White and Fun All Over

Black-and-white prints combined with
bright novelty prints will entertain babies and toddlers alike.

PROJECT RATING: EASY
Size: 41" × 47"
Blocks: 30 (6") Star blocks

MATERIALS

8 fat quarters★ black prints
8 fat quarters★ white prints
10 fat quarters★ bright prints
2¾ yards backing fabric
Crib-size quilt batting
★fat quarter = 18" × 20"

Cutting

Measurements include ¼" seam
allowances.

From each black print fat quarter, cut:

- 2 (3"-wide) strips. From strips, cut 8 (3" x 2") C rectangles for inner border and 5 (3" × 2¼") F rectangles for binding.
- 1 (2⅞"-wide) strip. From strip, cut 4 (2⅞") squares. Cut squares in half diagonally to make 8 half-square A triangles.

- 1 (2½"-wide) strip. From strip, cut 8 (2½") B squares.

From remainders of black prints, cut:

- 2 (4½") E squares for corners.

From each white fat quarter, cut:

- 1 (3"-wide) strip. From strip, cut 5 (3" × 2¼") F rectangles for binding.
- 1 (2⅞"-wide) strip. From strip, cut 4 (2⅞") squares. Cut squares in half diagonally to make 8 half-square A triangles.
- 1 (2½"-wide) strip. From strip, cut 8 (2½") B squares.

From remainders of white prints, cut:

- 2 (4½") E squares for corners.

From each bright print fat quarter, cut:

- 1 (4½"-wide) strip. From strip, cut 5 (4½" × 3½") D rectangles.
- 1 (2⅞"-wide) strip. From strip, cut 6 (2⅞") squares. Cut squares in half diagonally to make 12 half-square A triangles.
- 2 (2½"-wide) strips. From strips, cut 3 (2½") B squares.

Block Assembly

1. Choose a matching set of 4 black A triangles and 4 black B squares and a matching set of 4 bright A triangles and 1 bright B square.

2. Join 1 bright A triangle and 1 black A triangle as shown in *Triangle-Square Diagrams*. Make 4 triangle-squares.

Triangle-Square Diagrams

3. Referring to *Block Assembly Diagram,* lay out triangle-squares, black print B squares, and bright print B square. Join into rows; join rows to complete 1 Block A *(Block A Diagram)*. Make 15 Block A.

Block Assembly Diagram

Block A Diagram

4. In the same manner, make 1 Block B, using 4 matching white print A triangles, 4 white print B squares, 4 matching bright print A triangles, and 1 bright print B square *(Block B Diagram)*. Make 15 Block B.

Block B Diagram

Quilt Assembly

1. Lay out blocks as shown in *Quilt Top Assembly Diagram*. Join into rows; join rows to complete quilt center.

2. Join 15 black C rectangles to make 1 side inner border. Make 2 side inner borders. Trim side inner borders to 36½". Join to sides of quilt center.

3. Join 14 black C rectangles to make top inner border. Repeat for bottom inner border. Trim borders to 33½". Join to quilt center.

4. Join 13 bright D rectangles as shown to make 1 side outer border. Make 2 side outer borders. Join to sides of quilt.

5. In a similar manner, join 11 bright D rectangles to make top outer border. Repeat for bottom outer border.

6. Referring to *Quilt Top Assembly Diagram,* add 1 black E square and 1 white E square to top and bottom borders. Add borders to quilt.

Finishing

1. Divide backing into 2 (1⅜-yard) lengths. Cut 1 piece in half lengthwise to make 2 narrow panels. Join 1 narrow panel to wider panel. Seam will run horizontally. Remaining panel is extra and can be used to make a hanging sleeve.

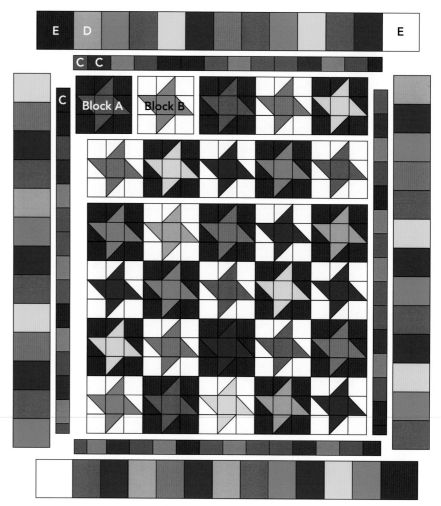

Quilt Top Assembly Diagram

2. Layer backing, batting, and quilt top; baste. Quilt as desired. Quilt shown was quilted with feather designs in the blocks and outer border *(Quilting Diagram)*.

3. Join F rectangles end to end, alternating black and white, to make 1 continuous piece for straight-grain French-fold binding. Add binding to quilt.

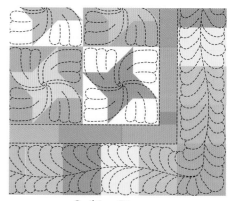

Quilting Diagram

DESIGNER

Linda Bowlin enjoys making quilts using traditional blocks with lots of color. She designed *Black & White and Fun All Over* for her first grandchild. A first grade teacher for 32 years, Linda knows what catches the eye of a youngster!

SIZE OPTIONS

	Table Topper (23" × 35")	Throw (65" × 77")	Twin (65" × 95")
Blocks	8	99	126
Setting	2 × 4	9 × 11	9 × 14

MATERIALS

Black Prints	4 fat eighths★★	13 fat quarters★	16 fat quarters★
White Prints	4 fat eighths★★	13 fat quarters★	16 fat quarters★
Bright Print	8 fat eighths★★	17 fat quarters★	21 fat quarters★
Backing Fabric	¾ yard	4 yards	5½ yards
Batting	Crib-size	Twin-size	Queen-size

CUTTING

Black Inner Border C Rectangles	32	100	114
Bright Outer Border D Rectangles	34	84	96
Black Binding E Rectangles	24	57	64
White Binding E Rectangles	24	57	64

★fat quarter = 18" × 20"

★★fat eighth = 9" × 20"

WEB EXTRA
Go to FonsandPorter.com/blackwhitesizes to download *Quilt Top Assembly Diagrams* for these size options.

TRIED & TRUE

Create a country look with fabrics such as these from the Wildrose collection by Brannock and Patek for Moda. ❋

Lions & Tigers & Zebras, Oh My!

Wild critters peek out from their hiding places to surprise your little one.

PROJECT RATING: INTERMEDIATE

Size: 41½" × 41½"

MATERIALS

1 yard animal print

1 fat quarter★★ green print #1

1 fat quarter★★ green print #2

1 fat quarter★★ white print

¾ yard blue print

1 yard orange print

1 fat eighth★ orange solid

7½" square template plastic

2¾ yards backing fabric

Twin-size quilt batting

★fat eighth = 9" × 20"

★★fat quarter = 18" × 20"

Cutting

Measurements include ¼" seam allowances. Border strips are exact length needed. You may want to make them longer to allow for piecing variations.

From animal print, cut:

- 1 (11⅛"-wide) strip. From strip, cut 3 (11⅛") squares. Cut squares in half diagonally in both directions to make 12 side setting triangles (6 are extra).
- 6 (7½") squares **on point**. Lay template plastic square atop fabric, centering design. Draw around square; cut on drawn line.

> ### Sew **Smart**™
> Edges of squares are bias. Handle carefully to avoid stretching. —Liz

> ### Sew **Smart**™
> Squares will be placed on point. Pay attention to direction of animals when cutting squares. —Marianne

From green print #1 fat quarter, cut:

- 1 (6⅛"-wide) strip. From strip, cut 2 (6⅛") squares. Cut squares in half diagonally in both directions to make 8 quarter-square B triangles (2 are extra).
- 2 (4"-wide) strips. From strips, cut 6 (4") A squares.

From green print #2 fat quarter, cut:

- 1 (6⅛"-wide) strip. From strip, cut 2 (6⅛") squares. Cut squares in half diagonally in both directions to make 8 quarter-square B triangles (2 are extra).
- 2 (4"-wide) strips. From strips, cut 6 (4") A squares.

From white print fat quarter, cut:

- 3 (4"-wide) strips. From strips, cut 9 (4") A squares.

From blue print, cut:

- 1 (4"-wide) strip. From strip, cut 9 (4") A squares.
- 5 (3¼"-wide) strips. From strips, cut 2 (3¼" × 36½") side outer borders. Piece remaining strips to make 2 (3¼" × 42") top and bottom outer borders.

From orange print, cut:

- 5 (2¼"-wide) strips for binding.
- 9 (1½"-wide) strips. From strips, cut 2 (1½" × 36½") top and bottom inner borders, 2 (1½" × 34½") side inner borders, 4 (1½" × 8¾") D sashing strips, and 32 (1½" × 7½") E sashing strips.

  NOTE: Sashing strips D are slightly oversized and will be trimmed when quilt top is complete.

From orange solid fat eighth, cut:

- 2 (1½"-wide) strips. From strips, cut 21 (1½") C squares.

Four Patch Unit Assembly

1. Lay out 1 green print #1 A square, 1 green print #2 A square, 1 blue print A square, and 1 white print A square as shown in *Four Patch Diagrams.*

Four Patch Diagrams

2. Join squares to make 1 Four Patch Unit. Make 6 Four Patch Units.

Triangle Unit Assembly

1. Lay out 1 blue print A square, 1 green print #1 B triangle, and 1 green print #2 B triangle. Join to make 1 Triangle Unit *(Triangle Unit Diagrams).* Make 3 Triangle Units.

Triangle Unit Diagrams

2. In the same manner, make 3 Triangle Units using 1 white print A square, 1 green print #2 B triangle, and 1 green print #1 B triangle.

Quilt Assembly

1. Lay out animal print squares, setting triangles, Four Patch Units, Triangle Units, sashing strips, and C squares as shown in *Quilt Top Assembly Diagram.*
2. Join into diagonal rows; join rows to complete quilt center. Trim sashing strips and squares even with edges of quilt center.
3. Add orange print side inner borders to quilt center. Add orange print top and bottom inner borders to quilt.
4. Repeat for blue print outer borders.

Finishing

1. Divide backing into 2 (1⅜-yard) lengths. Cut 1 piece in half lengthwise to make 2 narrow panels. Join 1 narrow panel to wider panel. Remaining panel is extra and can be used to make a hanging sleeve.

2. Layer backing, batting, and quilt top; baste. Quilt as desired. Quilt shown was quilted with a grid through the centers of the blocks and a diamond pattern in the outer border *(Quilting Diagram).*
3. Join 2¼"-wide orange print strips into 1 continuous piece for straight-grain French-fold binding. Add binding to quilt.

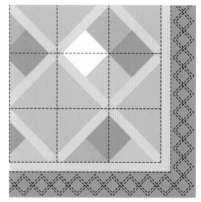

Quilting Diagram

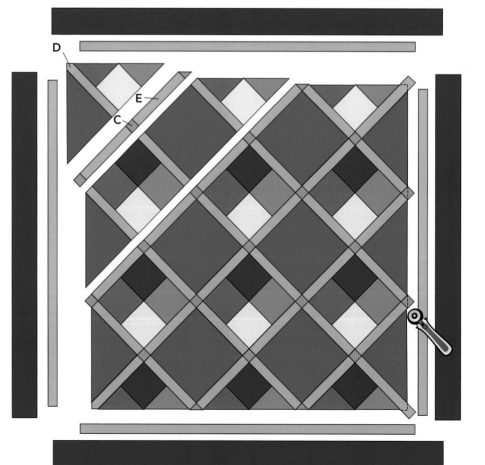

Quilt Top Assembly Diagram

SIZE OPTIONS

	Throw (64" × 75½")	Twin (64" × 86½")	Full (86½" × 98")
Four Patch Units	25	30	49
Setting	5 × 5	5 × 6	7 × 7

MATERIALS

Animal Print	2½ yards	3 yards	4½ yards
Green Print #1	⅝ yard	¾ yard	1 yard
Green Print #2	⅝ yard	¾ yard	1 yard
White Print	½ yard	⅝ yard	¾ yard
Orange Solid	¼ yard	¼ yard	⅜ yard
Blue Print	1¼ yards	1½ yards	1¾ yards
Orange Print	2 yards	2¼ yards	3⅛ yards
Backing Fabric	4½ yards	5¼ yards	7¾ yards
Batting	Twin-size	Full-size	King-size

WEB EXTRA
Go to FonsandPorter.com/ltzsizes to download *Quilt Top Assembly Diagrams* for these size options.

TRIED & TRUE

Our stylish sample features Twinkle Little

Star prints from Red Rooster Fabrics ✳

DESIGNER

Kristen Fisher enjoys using bright, bold colors in her quilts. She also creates mosaics from stained glass, which she says is a lot like assembling quilts. Kristen says both use pieces that don't look like much on their own, but when joined, make something beautiful and lasting.

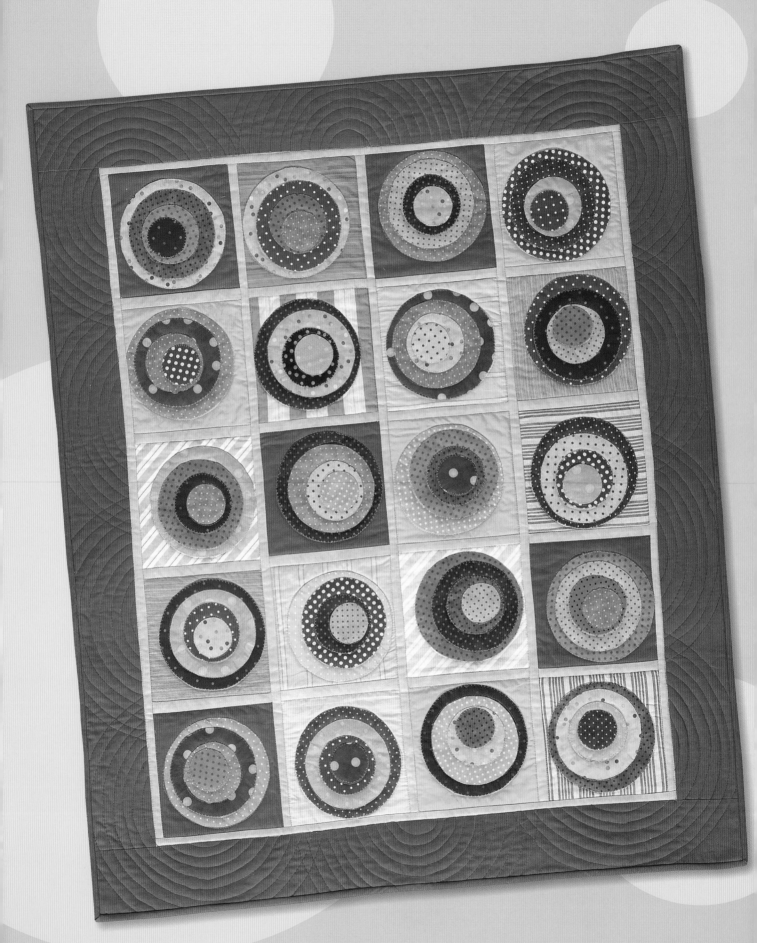

Dots for Tiny Tots

Gather a variety of dotted fabrics and
have fun arranging them to make this playful baby quilt.

PROJECT RATING: EASY
Size: 35½" × 42½"
Blocks: 20 (6½") blocks

MATERIALS

10 fat eighths★ assorted stripes and
  solids for background
10 fat quarters★★ assorted polka dot
  fabrics for blocks
⅜ yard light green solid
1 yard red solid
Paper-backed fusible web
1⅜ yards backing fabric
Crib-size quilt batting
★fat eighth = 9" × 20"
★★fat quarter = 18" × 20"

Cutting

Measurements include ¼" seam
allowances. Border strips are exact
length needed. You may want to make
them longer to allow for piecing
variations. Patterns for circles are on
page 41. **NOTE:** For instructions on
reducing bulk in fusible appliqué, see

Windowing Fusible Appliqué at www.
FonsandPorter.com/windowfuse.

From each fat eighth, cut:
• 1 (7"-wide) strip. From strip, cut 2
  (7") background squares.

From each fat quarter, cut:
• 2 A.
• 2 B.
• 2 C.
• 2 D.

From light green solid, cut:
• 11 (1"-wide) strips. From strips, cut
  5 (1" × 35") G sashing strips,
  2 (1" × 29") F sashing strips and
  16 (1" × 7") E sashing strips.

From red solid, cut:
• 4 (4"-wide) strips. From strips, cut
  4 (4" × 36") borders.
• 5 (2¼"-wide) strips for binding.

Block Assembly

1. Referring to *Block Diagram,* position
   1 A, 1 B, 1 C, and 1 D atop 1 background square. Fuse circles in place.
2. Using tan thread and blanket stitch,
   machine appliqué circles to complete
   1 block *(Block Diagram).* Make 20
   blocks.

Block Diagram

Quilt Assembly

1. Lay out blocks and sashing strips as
   shown in *Quilt Top Assembly Diagram*
   on page 40. Join into rows; join rows
   to complete quilt center.
2. Add red side borders to quilt center.
   Add red top and bottom borders to
   quilt.

Finishing

1. Layer backing, batting, and quilt top;
   baste. Quilt as desired. Quilt shown
   was outline quilted around each circle,
   quilted in the ditch around sashing,
   and has concentric arcs in the borders
   (Quilting Diagram on page 40).
2. Join 2¼"-wide red solid strips into
   1 continuous piece for straight-grain
   French-fold binding. Add binding to
   quilt.

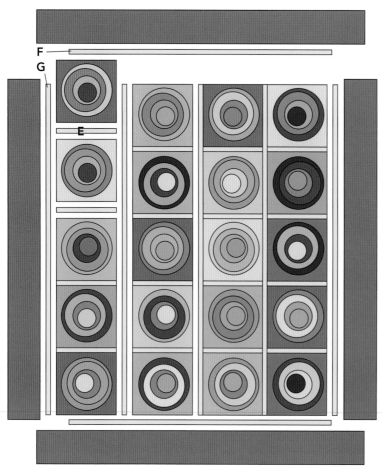

Quilt Top Assembly Diagram

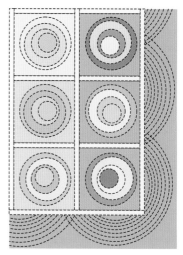

Quilting Diagram

DESIGNER

Sharon Smith of Minneapolis, Minnesota, calls designing quilt, punchneedle, and wool penny rug patterns her "therapy." She enjoys creating simple quilts and watching them evolve as she sews. ❊

TRIED & TRUE

Fabrics from the Shade Cascade collection by Blank give blocks a more grown-up look.

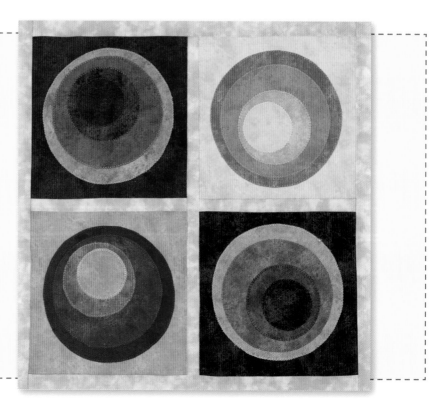

SIZE OPTION

Table Runner (21½" × 35½")	
Blocks	8
Setting	2 × 4

MATERIALS

Stripes and Solids	4 fat eighths
Dot Fabrics	8 fat eighths
Light Green Solid	¼ yard
Red Solid	⅞ yard
Backing Fabric	¾ yard
Batting	Craft-size

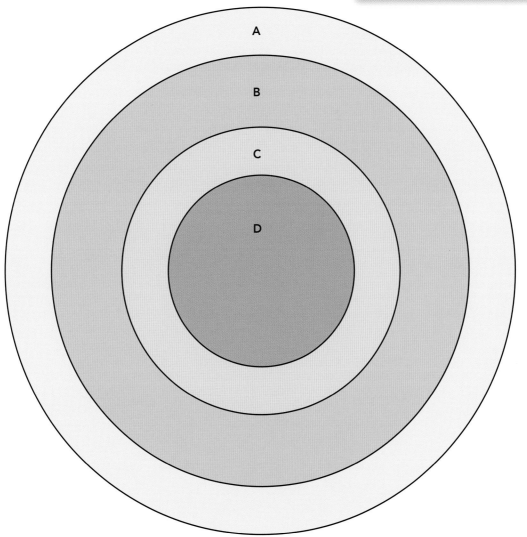

Circle of Life

A friend's antique quilt inspired Deb York to design this charming baby quilt, which she finished in time for the birth of her first grandchild. To make the circles using a quick and easy appliqué method, see *Sew Easy: Interfacing Appliqué* on page 45.

PROJECT RATING: INTERMEDIATE

Size: 36" × 54"

Blocks: 15 (7") blocks

MATERIALS

NOTE: Instructions for appliqué method using fusible interfacing are in *Sew Easy: Interfacing Appliqué* on page 45.

15 fat eighths★ assorted 1930s reproduction prints in red, yellow, green, blue, and pink for appliqué, sashing squares, and borders

1½ yards white print for block backgrounds and borders

1 yard red solid for sashing and binding

Lightweight fusible interfacing OR paper-backed fusible web

1¾ yards backing fabric

Crib-size quilt batting

★fat eighth = 9" × 20"

Cutting

Measurements include ¼" seam allowances. Border strips are exact length needed. You may want to make them longer to allow for piecing variations. Pattern for circle is on page 44. Follow manufacturer's instructions for using fusible web or fusible interfacing.

From each fat eighth, cut:

• 1 (2"-wide) strip. From strip, cut 9 (2") A squares.

• 5 Circles. **(Do not cut circles if using interfacing appliqué method.)**

From white print, cut:

• 3 (7½"-wide) strips. From strips, cut 15 (7½") background squares.

• 2 (2½"-wide) strips. From strips, cut 2 (2½" × 30½") top and bottom inner borders.

• 8 (2"-wide) strips. Piece strips to make 2 (2" × 51½") side outer borders, 2 (2" × 44½") side inner borders, and 2 (2" × 36½") top and bottom outer borders.

From red solid, cut:

• 5 (2¼"-wide) strips for binding.

• 8 (2"-wide) strips. From strips, cut 38 (2" × 7½") sashing strips.

Block Assembly

1. Position 5 Circles on white print background square as shown in *Block Diagram*. Fuse circles in place.

Block Diagram

2. Blanket stitch around circles using red thread to complete block *(Blanket Stitch Diagram)*. Make 15 blocks.

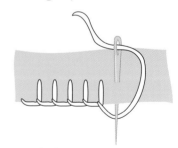

Blanket Stitch Diagram

Pieced Border Assembly

1. Join 32 A squares to make 1 side middle border. Make 2 side middle borders.

2. In the same manner, join 22 A squares to make top middle border. Repeat for bottom middle border.

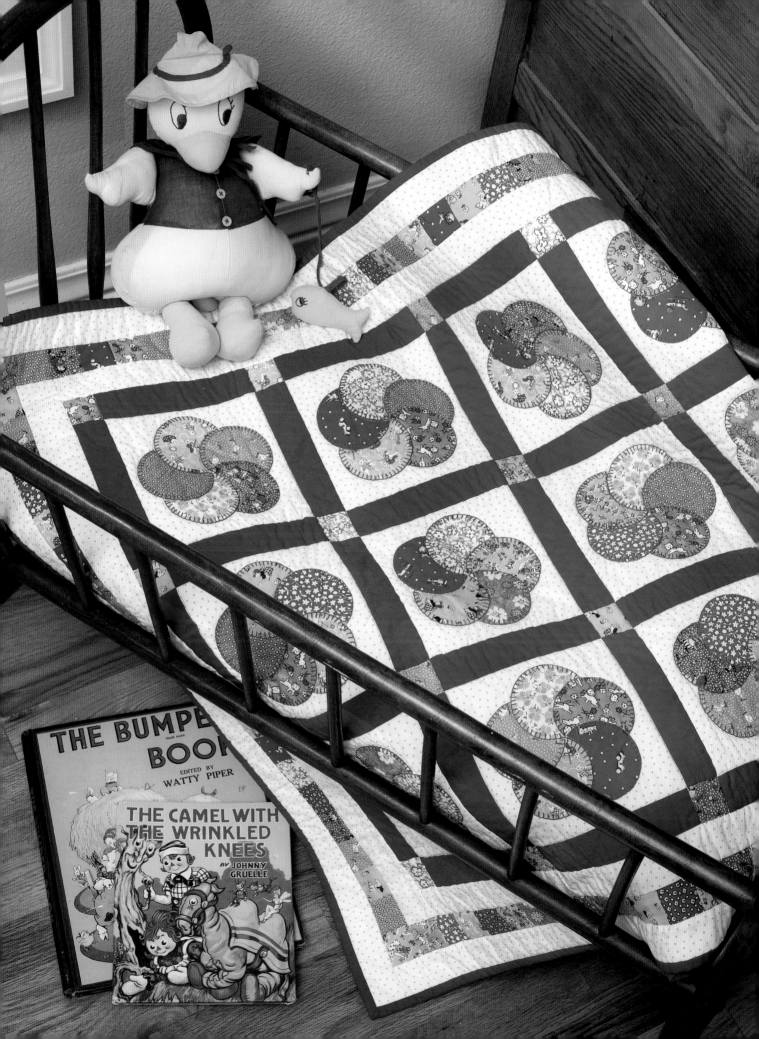

Quilt Assembly

1. Lay out blocks, red sashing strips, and 24 A squares as shown in *Quilt Top Assembly Diagram*.

2. Join into rows; join rows to complete quilt center.

3. Add white print side inner borders to quilt center. Add top and bottom inner borders to quilt.

4. Repeat for pieced middle borders and white print outer borders.

Finishing

1. Layer backing, batting, and quilt top; baste. Quilt as desired. Quilt shown was quilted in the ditch around blocks and borders, and outline quilted around circles.

2. Join 2¼"-wide red strips into 1 continuous piece for straight-grain French-fold binding. Add binding to quilt.

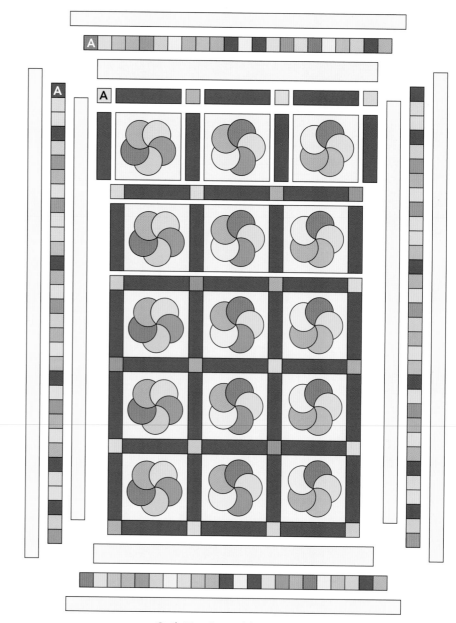

Quilt Top Assembly Diagram

TRIED & TRUE

Create a delicate watercolor effect with fabrics such as these from the Rosewater collection by P&B Textiles.

DESIGNER

Deb York learned quilting from her grandmother. She often draws inspiration for a project from a picture or pattern and then alters it to suit her own taste. Deb and her husband live in Adel, Iowa. ✳

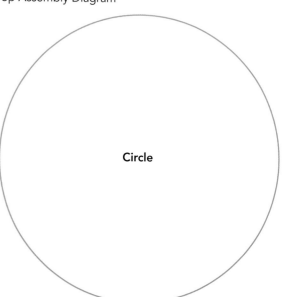

Circle

Interfacing Appliqué

For large shapes with fairly smooth edges, this appliqué technique works well. Fusing pieces to the background eliminates the need for basting.

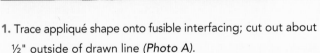
A

B

C

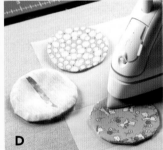
D

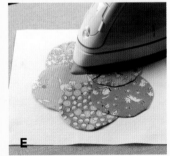
E

1. Trace appliqué shape onto fusible interfacing; cut out about ½" outside of drawn line (*Photo A*).
2. Position interfacing atop appliqué with fusible side of interfacing against right side of fabric. Stitch on drawn line through both layers (*Photo B*).
3. Trim away excess fabric, leaving a ¼" seam allowance. Cut a slit in interfacing to turn appliqué piece (*Photo C*).

4. Turn piece right side out, place on non-stick appliqué pressing sheet, and press shape flat (*Photo D*).
5. Lay out pieces on background fabric and fuse in place (*Photo E*).
6. Appliqué pieces to background using either a hand or machine stitch.

Sew Smart™
For curved pieces, clip curves OR trim seam allowance with pinking shears to make the piece lie flat when it is turned right side out. —Liz

QUILT BY **Magaret J. Miller**.
MACHINE QUILTED BY **Wanda Rains**.

Stars for My Little One

Margaret Miller's careful placement of pattern and color gives the viewer many different elements to see. Use Margaret's special templates to cut the shapes—see *Sew Easy: Making Pieced Rectangles* on page 53.

PROJECT RATING: CHALLENGING
Size: 51" × 51"
Blocks:
13 (12") Pinwheel blocks

NOTE: Fabrics in the quilt shown are Java Batiks by Galaxy Fabrics.

NOTE: Refer to *Sew Easy: Making Pieced Rectangles* on page 53 for cutting E base and side triangles and left-facing and right-facing triangles.

MATERIALS

NOTE: Fabrics are marbled prints unless otherwise stated.

½ yard light turquoise
⅜ yard dark turquoise
1 yard multicolor print for blocks and binding
⅝ yard dark blue/purple
½ yard blue/green
⅝ yard bright red
¼ yard dark red
¼ yard yellow
1 yard orange
1 yard purple dot print
⅜ yard olive
Template material
AnglePlay™ Templates Set 1 (optional)
3¼ yards backing fabric
Twin-size quilt batting

> ### Sew **Smart**™
> Edges of cut pieces may be on the bias. Handle carefully to avoid stretching. —Liz

Cutting

Measurements include ¼" seam allowances. Patterns for A, B, C, and E are on page 52.

From light turquoise, cut:
- 2 (6¾"-wide) strips. From strips, cut 36 right-facing B triangles.

From dark turquoise, cut:
- 2 (4¾"-wide) strips. From strips, cut 36 right-facing C triangles.

From multicolor print, cut:
- 1 (4¾"-wide) strip. From strip, cut 16 left-facing C triangles.
- 3 (3⅞"-wide) strips. From 1 strip, cut 16 E base triangles. From remaining strips, cut 16 (3⅞") squares. Cut squares in half diagonally to make 32 half-square F triangles.
- 6 (2¼"-wide) strips for binding.

From dark blue/purple, cut:
- 4 (4½"-wide) strips. From strips, cut 36 (4½" × 3½") D rectangles and 2 (3⅞") squares. Cut squares in half diagonally to make 4 half-square F triangles.

From blue/green, cut:
- 1 (4¾"-wide) strip. From strip, cut 8 right-facing C triangles.
- 2 (3⅞"-wide) strips. From strips, cut 12 (3⅞") squares. Cut squares in half diagonally to make 24 half-square F triangles.

From bright red, cut:
- 1 (7") square. Cut square in half diagonally in both directions to make 4 quarter-square H triangles.
- 1 (6¾"-wide) strip. From strip, cut 16 E side triangles.

- 1 (5½") square. Cut square in half diagonally in both directions to make 4 quarter-square G triangles.

From dark red, cut:
- 1 (4¾"-wide) strip. From strip, cut 4 right-facing C triangles.

From yellow, cut:
- 1 (6¾"-wide) strip. From strip, cut 16 right-facing E triangles.

From orange, cut:
- 1 (9¾"-wide) strip. From strip, cut 1 (9¾") square, 1 (5½") square, and 2 (5⅛") squares. Cut 9¾" square in half diagonally in both directions to make 4 quarter-square L triangles. Cut 5½" square in half diagonally in both directions to make 4 quarter-square G triangles. Cut 5⅛" squares in half diagonally to make 4 half-square K triangles.
- 1 (6¾"-wide) strip. From strip, cut 8 left-facing B triangles.
- 1 (4¾"-wide) strip. From strip, cut 8 right-facing A triangles and 8 right-facing C triangles.
- 1 (3⅞"-wide) strip. From strip, cut 8 (3⅞") squares. Cut squares in half diagonally to make 16 half-square F triangles.

From purple dot print, cut:
- 1 (7"-wide) strip. From strip, cut 1 (7") square and 2 (4⅛") squares. Cut 7" square in half diagonally in both directions to make 4 quarter-square H triangles. Cut 4⅛" squares in half diagonally in both directions to make 8 quarter-square J triangles.
- 1 (6⅞"-wide) strip. From strip, cut 4 (6⅞") squares. Cut squares in half diagonally to make 8 half-square I triangles.
- 2 (6¾"-wide) strips. From strips, cut 36 right-facing B triangles and 8 left-facing B triangles.

- 1 (5½"-wide) strip. From strip, cut 1 (5½") square and 8 right-facing A triangles. Cut square in half diagonally in both directions to make 4 quarter-square G triangles.

From olive, cut:
- 2 (4¾"-wide) strips. From strips, cut 32 right-facing C triangles.

NOTE: Refer to Color Key when making blocks.

	light turquoise
	dark turquoise
	multicolor print
	dark blue/purple
	blue/green
	bright red
	dark red
	yellow
	orange
	purple dot
	olive

Color Key

Block 1 Assembly

1. Lay out 1 light turquoise right-facing B triangle, 1 purple dot right-facing B triangle, 1 dark red right-facing C triangle, 1 dark turquoise right-facing C triangle, and 1 dark blue/purple D rectangle as shown in *Block 1 Unit Assembly Diagrams*. Join to make 1 Block 1 Unit *(Block 1 Unit Diagram)*. Make 4 Block 1 Units.

Block 1 Unit Assembly Diagrams

Block 2 Unit Assembly Diagrams

Block 3 Unit Diagram

2. Lay out 4 Block 3 Units as shown in *Block 3 Assembly Diagram*. Join into rows; join rows to complete 1 Block 3 *(Block 3 Diagram)*. Make 8 Block 3.

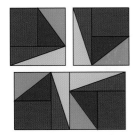

Block 1 Unit Diagram

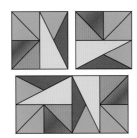

Block 2 Unit Diagram

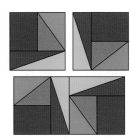

Block 3 Assembly Diagram

2. Lay out Block 1 Units as shown in *Block 1 Assembly Diagram*. Join into rows; join rows to complete 1 Block 1 *(Block 1 Diagram)*.

Block 1 Assembly Diagram

Block 2 Assembly Diagram

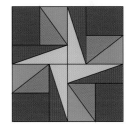

Block 3 Diagram

Side Unit Assembly

1. Lay out 1 orange right-facing C triangle, 1 blue/green right-facing C triangle, 1 orange left-facing B triangle, 1 purple dot left-facing B triangle, and 2 multicolor left-facing C triangles as shown in *Unit 1 Assembly Diagrams*. Join to complete 1 Unit 1 *(Unit 1 Diagram)*. Make 8 Unit 1.

Block 1 Diagram

Block 2 Assembly

1. Lay out 1 yellow right-facing E triangle, 1 bright red side E triangle, 1 multicolor base E triangle, 2 multicolor F triangles, 1 blue/green F triangle, and 1 orange F triangle as shown in *Block 2 Unit Assembly Diagrams*. Join to make 1 Block 2 Unit *(Block 2 Unit Diagram)*. Make 16 Block 2 Units.

2. Lay out 4 Block 2 Units as shown in *Block 2 Assembly Diagram*. Join into rows; join rows to complete 1 Block 2 *(Block 2 Diagram)*. Make 4 Block 2.

Block 2 Diagram

Block 3 Assembly

1. Lay out 1 light turquoise right-facing B triangle, 1 purple dot right-facing B triangle, 1 dark turquoise right-facing C triangle, 1 olive right-facing C triangle, and 1 dark blue/purple D rectangle as shown in *Block 3 Unit Assembly Diagrams*. Join to make 1 Block 3 Unit *(Block 3 Unit Diagram)*. Make 32 Block 3 Units.

Block 3 Unit Assembly Diagrams

Unit 1 Assembly Diagrams

Unit 1 Diagram

2. Lay out 1 orange right-facing A triangle, 1 purple dot right-facing A triangle, 1 bright red H triangle, and 1 purple dot J triangle as shown in *Unit 2 Assembly Diagrams*. Join to complete 1 Unit 2 *(Unit 2 Diagram)*. Make 4 Unit 2.

Unit 2 Assembly Diagrams

Unit 2 Diagram

3. Lay out 1 purple dot I triangle, 1 blue/green F triangle, and 1 purple dot G triangle as shown in *Unit 3 Assembly Diagrams*. Join to complete 1 Unit 3 *(Unit 3 Diagram)*. Make 4 Unit 3.

Unit 3 Assembly Diagrams

Unit 3 Diagram

4. Lay out 1 each Units 1, 2, and 3 as shown in *Side Unit Assembly Diagram*. Join to complete 1 Side Unit 1 *(Side Unit 1 Diagram)*. Make 4 Side Unit 1.

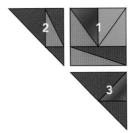

Side Unit Assembly Diagram

Side Unit 1 Diagram

5. In the same manner, make 4 Side Unit 2 as shown in *Side Unit 2 Diagrams*, using purple dot H triangle for Unit 2 and bright red G triangle for Unit 3.

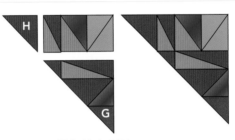

Side Unit 2 Diagrams

Corner Unit Assembly

1. Lay out 1 orange L triangle, 1 orange K triangle, 1 orange G triangle, and 1 dark blue/purple F triangle as shown in *Corner Unit Assembly Diagrams*.

Corner Unit Assembly Diagrams

2. Join to complete 1 Corner Unit *(Corner Unit Diagram)*. Make 4 Corner Units.

Corner Unit Diagram

Quilt Assembly

1. Lay out blocks, Side Units, and Corner Units as shown in *Quilt Top Assembly Diagram*.

2. Join into diagonal rows; join rows to complete quilt top.

Finishing

1. Divide backing into 2 (1⅝-yard) lengths. Join panels lengthwise.

2. Layer backing, batting, and quilt top; baste. Quilt as desired. Quilt shown was quilted with an allover swirl design *(Quilting Diagram)*.

3. Join 2¼"-wide multicolor print strips into 1 continuous piece for straight-grain French-fold binding. Add binding to quilt.

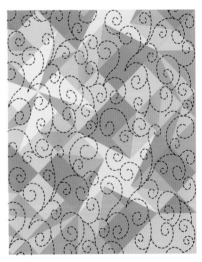

Quilting Diagram

Quilt Top Assembly Diagram

DESIGNER

Margaret J. Miller is the inventor of the AnglePlay™ templates, which make cutting and sewing the long triangle a breeze and bring new life to pieced blocks and quilts! She is an author, teacher, pattern designer, and studio quiltmaker, known for her use of strong colors. Her workshops and presentations are filled with humor, enthusiasm, and encouragement for quilters to "reach for the unexpected" in their contemporary quilts. When not traveling to teach, Margaret lives in the Pacific Northwest, where she savors sunny days and views of the Olympic Mountains that help her keep everything in perspective.

Contact her at:

Miller Quilts, Inc. • PO Box 4039 • Bremerton, WA 98311 • (360)698-2523

www.millerquilts.com ✳

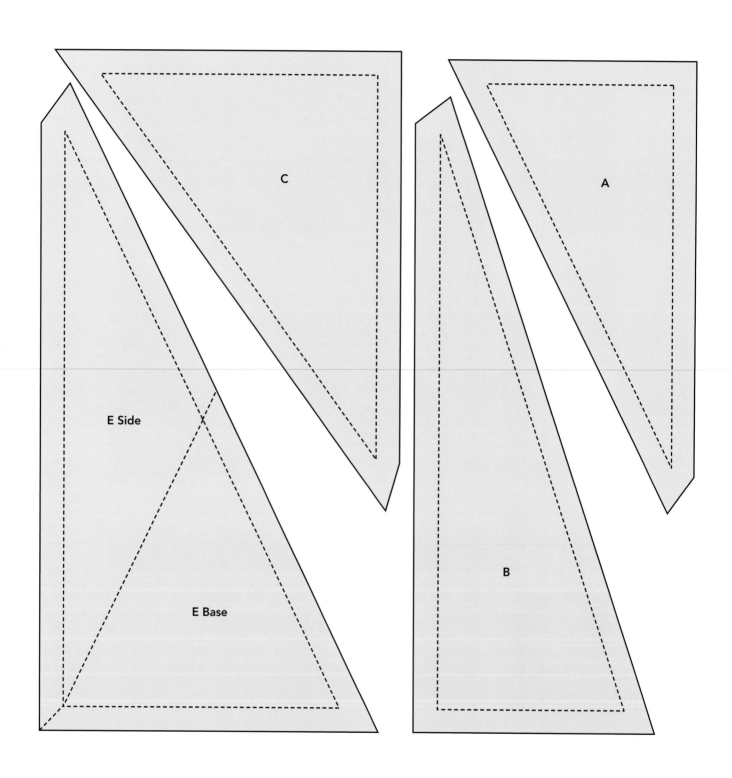

Making Pieced Rectangles

Piecing rectangles for the blocks in *Stars for My Little One* is a bit challenging. Follow these steps to guide you through the process

Cutting Triangles

Cut with fabrics right side up. Pay attention to the direction of the diagonal in your block when cutting left-facing and right-facing triangles *(Photo A)*.

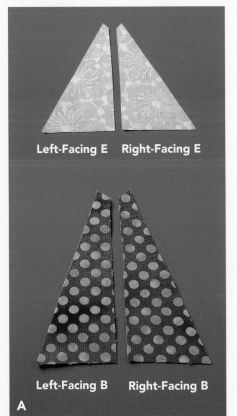

Left-Facing E   Right-Facing E

Left-Facing B   Right-Facing B

A

Making Pieced Triangles

You will "rough cut" the two pieces, sew them together, then reposition template on sewn fabrics, aligning the diagonal line on template with the seam.

1. To cut side triangle, place longest side of right-facing E triangle template on straight grain of fabric, ½" away from raw edge. Cut two-thirds of the way along the diagonal. Turn template over, align base of triangle and diagonal line ½" away from raw edges. Cut other side *(Photo B)*.

2. To cut base triangle, place base side of right-facing E triangle template on straight grain of fabric, ½" away from raw edge. Cut two-thirds of the way along the diagonal. Turn template over, align base of triangle and diagonal line ½" away from raw edges. Cut other side *(Photo C)*.

3. Join side triangle and base triangle along diagonal seam; press seam open. Place right-facing E triangle template on pieced triangle, aligning diagonal line on template with seam. Trim to size *(Photo D)*.

B

C

D

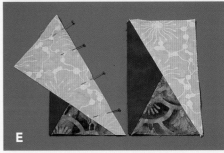

E

Making Pieced Rectangles

Join right-facing E triangle to pieced right-facing E triangle to complete pieced rectangle *(Photo E)*.

Basketweave

Love of Quilting editor Jean Nolte and her mother, Betty Hufford, teamed up to make this dynamic baby quilt. The construction is not difficult, but it is a bit tricky. Be sure to read all the assembly instructions before you begin piecing.

PROJECT RATING: INTERMEDIATE

Size: 48" × 60"

MATERIALS

1 yard pink print
⅞ yard yellow print
⅞ yard blue print
¾ yard green print
1 yard purple print
3 yards backing fabric
Twin-size quilt batting

Sew **Smart**™

Choose a dark fabric for the B squares so they recede into the background and let the other fabrics appear to weave over it. —Liz

Cutting

Measurements include ¼" seam allowances. Border strips are exact length needed. You may want to make them longer to allow for piecing variations

From pink print, cut:

• 6 (4½"-wide) strips. From 4 strips, cut 49 (4½" × 2½") A rectangles. Piece remaining strips to make 1 (4½" × 44½") top border.

• 1 (3½"-wide) strip. From strip, cut 14 (3½" × 2½") C rectangles.

From yellow print, cut:

• 6 (4½"-wide) strips. From 4 strips, cut 54 (4½" × 2½") A rectangles. Piece remaining strips to make 1 (4½" × 56½") side border.

From blue print, cut:

• 5 (4½"-wide) strips. From 3 strips, cut 40 (4½ " × 2½") A rectangles. Piece remaining strips to make 1 (4½" × 56½") side border.

• 1 (3½-wide) strip. From strip, cut 16 (2½" × 3½") C rectangles.

From green print, cut:

• 5 (4½"-wide) strips. From 3 strips, cut 48 (4½" × 2½") A rectangles. Piece remaining strips to make 1 (4½" × 44½") bottom border.

From purple print, cut:

• 6 (2¼"-wide) strips for binding.

• 13 (1½"-wide) strips. From 8 strips, cut 192 (1½") B squares. Piece remaining strips to make 2 (1½" × 50½") side inner borders and 2 (1½" × 40½") top and bottom inner borders.

Quilt Assembly

NOTE: Piecing this quilt uses a special technique. Read all instructions before beginning to sew.

1. Using a partial seam as shown in *Unit 1 Diagrams* on page 56, join 1 purple print B square to corner of 1 green print A rectangle. Repeat for remaining corners to complete Unit 1. Make 48 Unit 1.

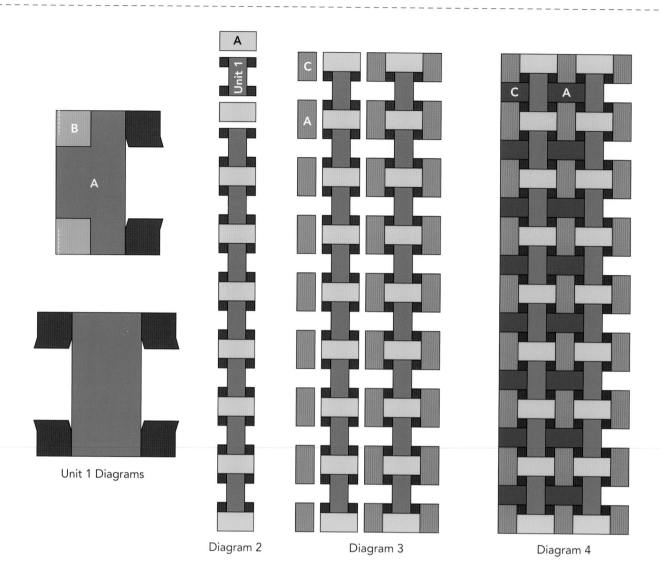

Unit 1 Diagrams

Diagram 2   Diagram 3   Diagram 4

2. Join 9 yellow print A rectangles and 8 Unit 1 to make a row as shown in *Diagram 2*. Make 6 rows.

3. Join rows using pink print A and C rectangles as shown in *Diagram 3*. You will have a lattice with holes in it.

4. Add blue print A and C rectangles in the holes in the lattice *(Diagram 4)*. Referring to *Diagram 5,* stitch the long sides of the blue rectangles to the pink print rectangle/purple squares (seam #1), then complete the partial seams on B squares from step #1, connecting the short sides of the blue rectangles to the green print A rectangles (seam #2).

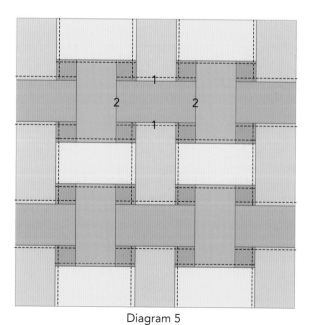

Diagram 5

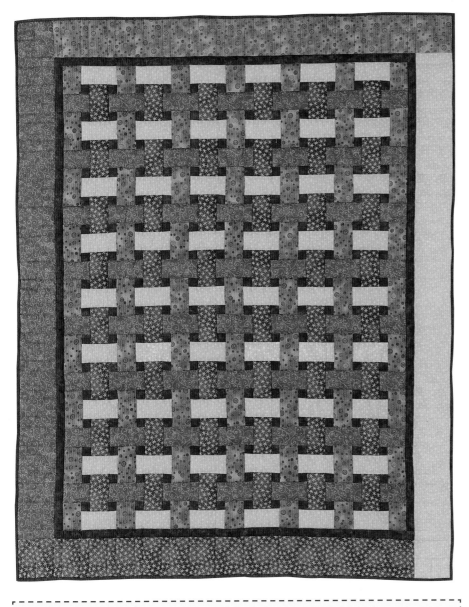

5. Add purple print side inner borders to quilt center. Add top and bottom inner borders to quilt.

6. Using a partial seam, join pink print top border to quilt. Start stitching at left side edge and stop 1" before right side edge.

7. Add blue print left side border, green print bottom border, and yellow print right side border to quilt.

8. Complete partial seam.

Finishing

1. Divide backing fabric into 2 (1½-yard) pieces. Join panels lengthwise. Seam will run horizontally.

2. Layer backing, batting, and quilt top; baste. Quilt as desired. Quilt shown was quilted in the ditch around all pieces and has parallel lines in outer border.

3. Join 2¼"-wide purple print strips into 1 continuous piece for straight-grain French-fold binding. Add binding to quilt.

Sew Smart™

To enhance the woven effect of this design, use a high-loft batting. The quilt shown has 2 layers of medium-loft batting. —Marianne

TRIED & TRUE

Spice up this design by using rich, bold prints such as these from the Texture Grafica Collection by Windham Fabrics.

Baby Blessings

The sayings printed on fabric are perfect for the centers of Log Cabin blocks.
The flannels make this baby quilt extra snuggly.

PROJECT RATING: EASY

Size: 39½" × 49½"

Blocks: 12 (10") Courthouse Steps blocks

MATERIALS

1¼ yards stripe for borders and block centers

½ yard coral print

½ yard green print

⅜ yard blue print

¾ yard yellow print #1

¼ yard yellow print #2

⅛ yard pink print #1

⅛ yard pink print #2

4½" square template plastic

2½ yards backing fabric

Crib-size quilt batting

NOTE: Flannels in the quilt shown are from the Little Blessings collection by Nancy Davis Murty for Andover Fabrics.

Sew **Smart**™

Because there are so many pieces which are similar in size, you may want to label them as you cut.
—Marianne

Cutting

Measurements include ¼" seam allowances. Border strips are exact length needed. You may want to make them longer to allow for piecing variations.

From stripe, cut:

- 4 (5¼"-wide) **lengthwise** strips, centering design on each. From strips, cut 2 (5¼" × 40½") side borders and 2 (5¼" × 30½") top and bottom borders.

From remaining stripe fabric, fussy cut:

- 12 (4½") block center squares. Place template plastic square atop fabric, centering design. Draw around template; cut on drawn line.

From coral print, cut:

- 6 (2"-wide) strips. From strips, cut:
  - 6 (2" × 10½") #4 pieces.
  - 6 (2" × 7½") #3 pieces.
  - 6 (2" × 7½") #2 pieces.
  - 6 (2" × 4½") #1 pieces.

From green print, cut:

- 1 (5¼"-wide) strip. From strip, cut 4 (5¼") border corner squares.
- 5 (2"-wide) strips. From strips, cut:
  - 5 (2" × 10½") #4 pieces.
  - 5 (2" × 7½") #3 pieces.
  - 5 (2" × 7½") #2 pieces.
  - 5 (2" × 4½") #1 pieces.

From blue print, cut:

- 5 (2"-wide) strips. From strips, cut:
  - 5 (2" × 10½") #4 pieces.
  - 5 (2" × 7½") #3 pieces.
  - 5 (2" × 7½") #2 pieces.
  - 5 (2" × 4½") #1 pieces.

From yellow print #1, cut:

- 5 (2½"-wide) strips for binding.
- 3 (2"-wide) strips. From strips, cut:
  - 3 (2" × 10½") #4 pieces.
  - 3 (2" × 7½") #3 pieces.
  - 3 (2" × 7½") #2 pieces.
  - 3 (2" × 4½") #1 pieces.

From yellow print #2, cut:
- 3 (2"-wide) strips. From strips, cut:
  - 3 (2" × 10½") #4 pieces.
  - 3 (2" × 7½") #3 pieces.
  - 3 (2" × 7½") #2 pieces.
  - 3 (2" × 4½") #1 pieces.

From pink print #1, cut:
- 1 (2"-wide) strip. From strip, cut:
  - 1 (2" × 10½") #4 pieces.
  - 1 (2" × 7½") #3 pieces.
  - 1 (2" × 7½") #2 pieces.
  - 1 (2" × 4½") #1 pieces.

From pink print #2, cut:
- 1 (2"-wide) strip. From strip, cut:
  - 1 (2" × 10½") #4 piece.
  - 1 (2" × 7½") #3 piece.
  - 1 (2" × 7½") #2 piece.
  - 1 (2" × 4½") #1 piece.

Block Assembly

1. Lay out block centers in 4 horizontal rows with 3 in each row. Beginning at top left corner, number block centers #1–#12 as shown in *Quilt Top Assembly Diagram.*

2. Choose 1 green print set of strips #1–#4 and 1 coral print set of strips #1–#4. Referring to *Block Diagram* for placement, add strips to block center in numerical order to complete block #1.

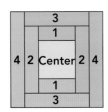

Block Diagram

3. In the same manner, make blocks #2–#12, referring to photo on page 61 and *Quilt Top Assembly Diagram* for color placement.

Quilt Top Assembly Diagram

Quilt Assembly

1. Lay out blocks as shown in *Quilt Top Assembly Diagram.* Join into rows; join rows to complete quilt center.

2. Add side borders to quilt center.

3. Add 1 green print border corner square to each end of top and bottom borders. Add borders to quilt.

Finishing

1. Divide backing into 2 (1¼-yard) lengths. Cut 1 piece in half lengthwise to make 2 narrow panels. Join 1 narrow panel to wider panel. Seam will run horizontally. Remaining panel is extra and can be used to make a hanging sleeve.

2. Layer backing, batting, and quilt top; baste. Quilt as desired. Quilt shown was quilted in the ditch and with loops and swirls *(Quilting Diagram).*

3. Join 2½"-wide yellow print strips into 1 continuous piece for straight-grain French-fold binding. Add binding to quilt. ✳

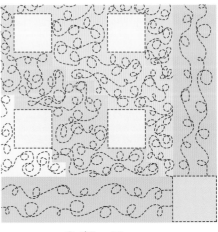

Quilting Diagram

WEB EXTRA
Visit our Web site at: FonsandPorter.com/ablesssizes to download more size options and
Quilt Top Assembly Diagrams for this quilt.

Daisy Dreams

Fanciful tossed daisies and happy colors are joined in a
bright mix in this darling crib quilt.

PROJECT RATING: INTERMEDIATE
Size: 48" × 48"
Blocks: 5 (12") Flower blocks
4 (12") pieced blocks

MATERIALS

¾ yard dark pink print for blocks,
appliqué, and outer border

⅝ yard pink floral print for blocks
and outer border

⅛ yard light pink print for blocks

1 fat quarter★ dark green print for
appliqué

⅛ yard green dot for blocks

⅛ yard light green print for blocks

⅝ yard green floral print for inner
border

¾ yard dark yellow print for blocks
and binding

¾ yard light yellow print for
appliqué blocks

Paper-backed fusible web

3 yards backing fabric

Twin-size quilt batting

★fat quarter = 18" × 20"

NOTE: Fabrics in the quilt shown are
from Clothworks.

Cutting

Measurements include ¼" seam allowances. Border strips are exact length
needed. You may want to make them
longer to allow for piecing variations.
Patterns for appliqué are on page 66.
Follow manufacturer's instructions for
using fusible web.

From dark pink print, cut:

• 3 (4⅞"-wide) strips. From strips, cut
20 (4⅞") squares. Cut squares in half
diagonally to make 40 half-square B
triangles.

• 1 (2½"-wide) strip. From strip, cut
16 (2½") A squares.

• 5 Flowers.

From pink floral print, cut:

• 3 (4⅞"-wide) strips. From strips, cut
20 (4⅞") squares. Cut squares in half
diagonally to make 40 half-square B
triangles.

• 1 (2½"-wide) strip for strip set.

From light pink print, cut:

• 1 (2½"-wide) strip for strip set.

From dark green print, cut:

• 5 Stems.

• 10 Leaves.

From green dot, cut:

• 1 (2½"-wide) strip for strip set.

• 5 Flower Centers.

From light green print, cut:

• 1 (2½"-wide) strip for strip set.

From green floral print, cut:

• 1 (4½"-wide) strip. From strip, cut
4 (4½") D squares.

• 4 (2½"-wide) strips. From strips cut,
2 (2½" × 40½") top and bottom inner
borders and 2 (2½" × 36½") side inner
borders.

From dark yellow print, cut:

• 4 (2½"-wide) strips. From strips, cut
16 (2½" × 8½") C rectangles.

• 6 (2¼"-wide) strips for binding.

From light yellow print, cut:

• 2 (12½"-wide) strips. From strips, cut
5 (12½") E squares.

Pieced Block Assembly

1. Join 1 green dot strip and 1 pink floral strip as shown in *Strip Set Diagram*. From strip set, cut 8 (4½"-wide) segments.

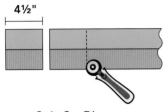

Strip Set Diagram

2. In the same manner, make a strip set using light pink print and light green print strips. From strip set, cut 8 (4½"-wide) segments.

3. Lay out 4 strip set segments, 4 dark yellow print C rectangles, and 4 dark pink print A squares as shown in *Pieced Block Assembly Diagram*. Join into rows; join rows to complete 1 block (*Pieced Block Diagram*). Make 4 pieced blocks.

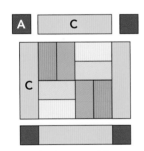

Pieced Block Assembly Diagram

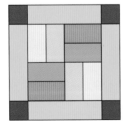

Pieced Block Diagram

Flower Block Assembly

1. Lay out 2 Leaves, 1 Stem, 1 Flower, and 1 Flower Center atop light yellow print E square as shown in *Flower Block Diagram*. Fuse pieces in place.

Flower Block Diagram

2. Machine blanket stitch around each appliqué piece using matching thread to complete 1 Flower block. Make 5 Flower blocks.

Border Assembly

1. Join 1 dark pink print B triangle and 1 pink floral B triangle as shown in *Triangle-Square Diagrams*. Make 40 triangle-squares.

Triangle-Square Diagrams

2. Lay out 10 triangle-squares as shown in *Quilt Top Assembly Diagram*. Join to complete 1 pieced border. Make 4 pieced borders.

Quilt Assembly

1. Lay out blocks as shown in *Quilt Top Assembly Diagram.*

2. Join blocks into rows; join rows to complete quilt center.

3. Add green floral side inner borders to quilt center. Add top and bottom inner borders to quilt.

4. Add pieced borders to sides of quilt.

5. Add 1 green floral D square to each end of remaining pieced borders. Add borders to top and bottom of quilt.

Finishing

1. Divide backing fabric into 2 (1½-yard) pieces. Cut 1 piece in half lengthwise to make 2 narrow panels. Join 1 narrow panel to wider panel. Press seam allowances toward narrow panel. Remaining panel is extra and can be used to make a hanging sleeve.

2. Layer backing, batting, and quilt top; baste. Quilt as desired. Quilt shown was quilted with an overall design of loops and leaves (*Quilting Diagram*).

3. Join 2¼"-wide dark yellow strips into 1 continuous piece for straight-grain French-fold binding. Add binding to quilt.

Quilting Diagram

Quilt Top Assembly Diagram

TRIED & TRUE

Substitute dark prints
for the patchwork and
a heartwarming red for
flower petals to give this
pattern a more
traditional feel. ✳

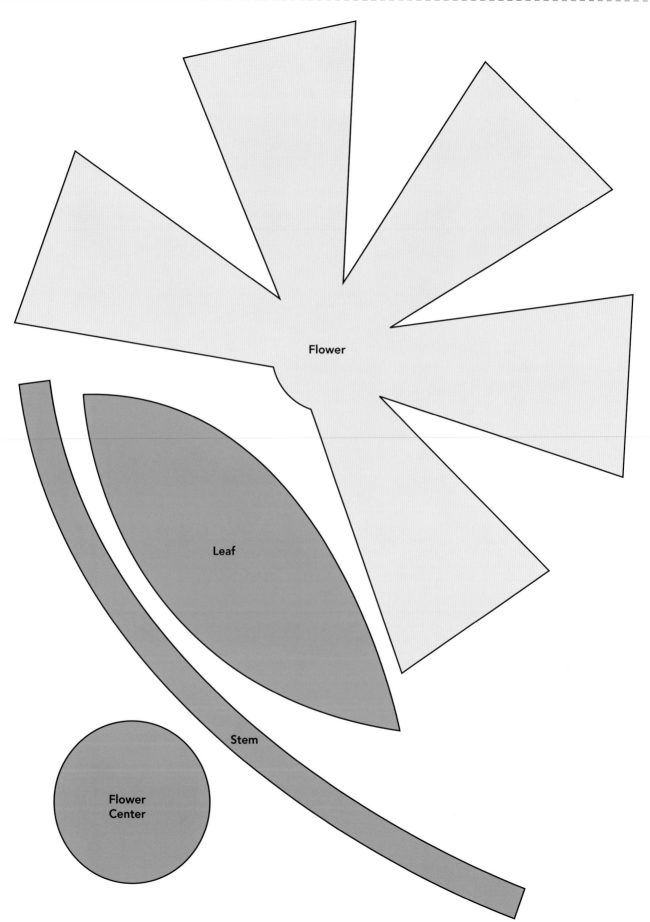

Flower

Leaf

Stem

Flower
Center

MADE BY **Cindy Hathaway**.
DESIGNED AND MACHINE QUILTED BY **Jean Nolte**.

Baby Friends

Start with a playful panel, add borders, and you'll have this baby quilt finished in no time! We made two—one for a boy and one for a girl.

PROJECT RATING: Easy
Size: 38" × 46"

MATERIALS

NOTE: Materials listed are for 1 quilt.
1 printed panel
1¼ yards blue or pink print for border and binding
1½ yards backing fabric
Crib-size quilt batting

NOTE: Fabrics in the quilt shown are from the Spring Fling collection by David Walker for Free Spirit Fabrics.

Cutting

Measurements include ¼" seam allowances. Border strips are exact length needed. You may want to make them longer to allow for piecing variations.

From printed panel fabric, cut:

• 1 (26½" × 34½") rectangle, centering design.

From blue or pink print, cut:

• 4 (6½"-wide) strips. From strips, cut 2 (6½" × 38½") top and bottom borders and 2 (6½" × 34½") side borders.

• 5 (2¼"-wide) strips for binding.

Quilt Assembly

1. Referring to *Quilt Top Assembly Diagram*, add side borders to quilt center. **NOTE:** For perfectly-fitting borders, refer to *Sew Easy: Borders That Fit* on page 71.

2. Add top and bottom borders to quilt.

Finishing

1. Layer backing, batting, and quilt top; baste. Quilt as desired. Quilt shown was quilted in the ditch and with straight parallel lines in center panel and border *(Quilting Diagram)*.

2. Join 2¼"-wide blue or pink print strips into 1 continuous piece for straight-grain French-fold binding. Add binding to quilt.

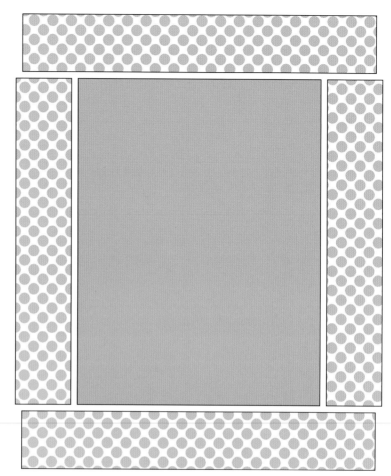

Quilt Top Assembly Diagram

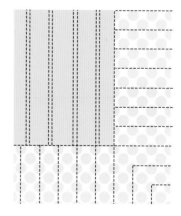

Quilting Diagram

Borders That Fit

Follow these simple instructions to make perfect borders every time.

1. Find the side dimensions of your quilt by measuring through the quilt center, not along the edges, since the edges may have stretched. Take 3 measurements and average them to determine the length to cut your borders. (Diagram A).

2. Attach side borders to quilt center by pinning them at the ends and the center, and easing in any fullness. If quilt edge is a bit longer than border, pin and sew with border on top. Machine feed dogs can ease in some fullness. Press seams toward borders.

3. Find the top and bottom dimensions of your quilt by measuring across the quilt and side borders (Diagram B). Cut borders this length.

4. Attach top and bottom borders to quilt, pinning at ends and center, and easing in any fullness. Press seams toward borders.

HELPFUL TIP

Use the following decimal conversions to calculate your quilt's measurements:

$\frac{1}{8}$" = .125 $\frac{5}{8}$" = .625

$\frac{1}{4}$" = .25 $\frac{3}{4}$" = .75

$\frac{3}{8}$" = .375 $\frac{7}{8}$" = .875

$\frac{1}{2}$" = .5

A _____

B _____

C _____

TOTAL _____

÷3 _____

AVERAGE
LENGTH _____

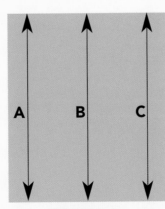

Diagram A

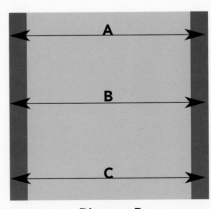

Diagram B

Little Lambs Eat Ivy

Stitch these adorable lambs to delight your little one. Soft colors and sweet lamb prints add to the charm of this baby quilt.

PROJECT RATING: INTERMEDIATE

Size: 36" × 47"

Blocks: 12 (7") Lamb blocks

MATERIALS

- 3 fat quarters★★ assorted yellow prints for block background
- 12 (6") squares assorted bright lamb prints for bodies
- 1 fat eighth★ black print for lamb features
- 4 fat eighths★ assorted bright solids in purple, pink, yellow, and blue for hearts
- 8 fat eighths★ assorted bright prints in purple, pink, yellow, blue, and green for inner border
- 1 fat eighth★ yellow check for sashing
- 1 fat quarter★★ green plaid for vine
- ¼ yard green print for middle border
- ¾ yard light blue print for outer border
- ⅝ yard white solid for fence
- ⅝ yard white print for sashing
- 5 (10") squares assorted green prints for ivy leaves
- ½ yard pastel stripe for binding
- Paper for foundations
- Paper-backed fusible web
- 1½ yards backing fabric
- Crib-size quilt batting
- ★fat eighth = 9" × 20"
- ★★fat quarter = 18" × 20"

Cutting

Measurements include ¼" seam allowances. Border strips are exact length needed. You may want to make them longer to allow for piecing variations. Patterns for appliqué shapes and foundations are on page 76. Follow manufacturer's instructions for using fusible web.

NOTE: For instructions on paper foundation piecing, see *Sew Easy: Paper Foundation Piecing* on page 77.

From each yellow print fat quarter, cut:

- 2 (7½"-wide) strips. From strips, cut 4 (7½") background squares.

From each bright lamb print, cut:

- 1 Body.

From black print, cut:
- 12 Heads.
- 12 Ears.
- 24 Legs.

From each bright print fat eighth, cut:
- 3 (1½"-wide) strips for strip sets.

From yellow check, cut:
- 4 (1½"-wide) strips. From strips, cut 8 (1½" × 7½") B rectangles.

From green plaid, cut:
- 14 (¾" × 12") bias strips.

From green print, cut:
- 4 (1"-wide) strips. From strips, cut 2 (1" × 38½") side middle borders and 2 (1" × 28½") top and bottom middle borders.

From light blue print, cut:
- 3 (2½"-wide) strips for strip sets.
- 5 (1½"-wide) strips. From 2 strips, cut 66 (1½" × 1") E rectangles. Remaining strips are for strip sets.
- 4 (1"-wide) strips. From strips, cut 132 (1") C squares.

From white solid, cut:
- 3 (4"-wide) strips. From strips, cut 66 (4" × 1½") D rectangles.
- 3 (1½"-wide) strips for strip sets.

From white print, cut:
- 1 (2½"-wide) strip. From strip, cut 18 (2½" × 2") A rectangles.

From assorted green prints, cut:
- 42 Large Leaves.
- 23 Small Leaves.

From pastel stripe, cut:
- 5 (2¼"-wide) strips for binding.

Block Assembly

1. Arrange 1 Body, 1 Head, 1 Ear, and 2 Legs on 1 yellow print background square. Fuse pieces in place; machine blanket stitch using matching thread to complete 1 Lamb block *(Lamb Block Diagram)*. Make 12 Lamb blocks.

Lamb Block Diagram

2. Trace 4 Large Heart foundations and 21 Small Heart foundations onto tracing paper.

3. Foundation piece Hearts in numerical order using assorted solid fabrics for heart pieces and white print for background pieces. For detailed instructions, see *Sew Easy: Paper Foundation Piecing* on page 77. Make 1 purple, 1 pink, 1 yellow, and 1 blue Large Heart *(Heart Block Diagram)*.

Heart Block Diagram

4. In the same manner, make 4 purple, 5 pink, 6 yellow, and 6 blue Small Hearts.

Pieced Inner Border Assembly

1. Join 2 (1½"-wide) assorted print strips as shown in *Strip Set #1 Diagram*. Make 12 Strip Set #1. From strip sets, cut 122 (1½"-wide) segments.

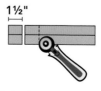

Strip Set #1 Diagram

2. Join 34 segments to make 1 side inner border as shown in *Quilt Top Assembly Diagram*. Make 2 side inner borders.

3. In the same manner, join 27 segments to make top inner border. Repeat for bottom inner border.

Outer Border Assembly

1. Referring to *Diagonal Seams Diagrams*, place 1 light blue print C square atop 1 white D rectangle, right sides facing. Stitch diagonally from corner to corner as shown. Trim ¼" beyond stitching. Press open to reveal triangle. Repeat for adjacent corner. Add 1 (1" × 1½") light blue print E rectangle to complete 1 Fence Unit *(Fence Unit Diagram)*. Make 66 Fence Units.

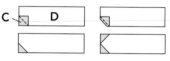

Diagonal Seams Diagrams

Fence Unit Diagram

2. Join 1 (1½"-wide) light blue print strip, 1 (1½"-wide) white strip, and 1 (2½"-wide) light blue print strip as shown in *Strip Set #2 Diagram*. Make 3 Strip Set #2. From strip sets, cut 70 (1½"-wide) segments.

Strip Set #2 Diagram

3. Referring to *Quilt Top Assembly Diagram*, join 19 Fence Units and 20 strip set #2 segments alternately to make 1 Side Outer border. Make 2 Side Outer borders.

4. In the same manner, join 14 Fence Units and 15 strip set #2 segments to make top outer border. Repeat for bottom outer border.

5. Fold green plaid bias strips in thirds, press, and hand baste folds in place to prepare vines for appliqué.

6. Referring to quilt photo on page 72 and *Quilt Top Assembly Diagram*, arrange bias strips on 1 side outer border to make a continuous curving vine. Remove a few stitches in seams to tuck in ends of bias strips (vine appears to go behind picket units). Re-sew seams. Topstitch vines close to edges with matching thread. Repeat for remaining borders.

7. Arrange assorted green print leaves on vines and machine appliqué using a small blanket stitch and matching thread.

8. Machine stitch tendrils on vines using green thread as shown in photo on page 72.

Quilt Assembly

1. Referring to *Quilt Top Assembly Diagram*, lay out Lamb blocks, Small Heart blocks, white print A rectangles, and yellow check B rectangles. Join into rows; join rows to complete quilt center.

2. Add side inner borders to quilt center. Add top and bottom inner borders to quilt.

3. Add green print side middle borders to quilt center. Add green print top and bottom middle borders to quilt.

4. Add side outer borders to quilt.

5. Trim ½" from each end of top and bottom outer borders. Join 1 Heart block to each end of borders. Add borders to quilt.

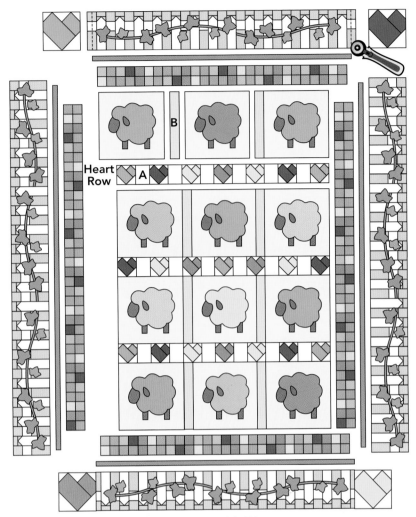

Quilt Top Assembly Diagram

Finishing

1. Layer backing, batting, and quilt top; baste. Quilt as desired. Quilt shown was quilted with swirls on the lambs, crosshatching and meandering in the background, egg and dart design in the pieced inner border, and ¼" echo quilting on the fence *(Quilting Diagram)*.

2. Join 2¼"-wide pastel stripe strips into 1 continuous piece for straight-grain French-fold binding. Add binding to quilt.

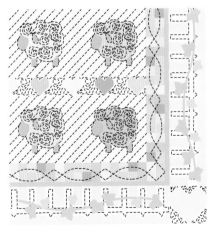

Quilting Diagram

DESIGNER

Janet Stone of Overland Park, Kansas, had been collecting sheep fabric for quite some time. When the opportunity to enter Fons & Porter's Baby Quilt Contest arose, she designed this adorable quilt. The idea for the border and the title came to Janet as she was humming the popular song "Mairzy Doats." ✳

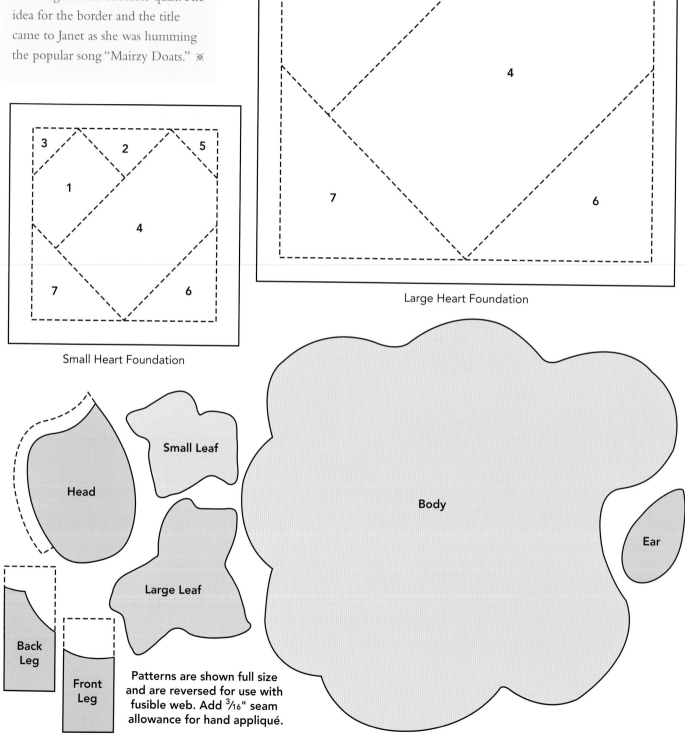

Large Heart Foundation

Small Heart Foundation

Head

Small Leaf

Large Leaf

Body

Ear

Back Leg

Front Leg

Patterns are shown full size and are reversed for use with fusible web. Add 3/16" seam allowance for hand appliqué.

Sew Easy™

Paper Foundation Piecing

Use this quick and easy method for the Heart blocks in *Little Lambs Eat Ivy.*

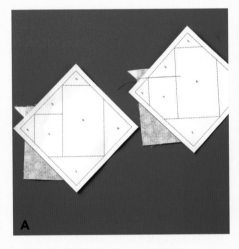

A

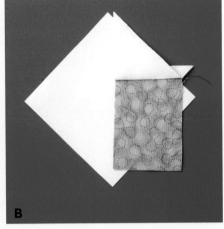

B

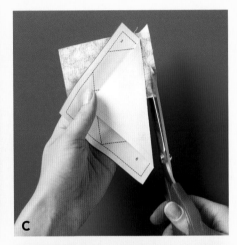

C

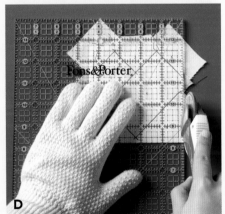

D

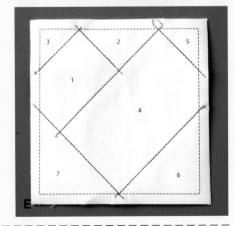

E

1. Using ruler and pencil, trace the outline of all shapes and the outer edge of the foundation pattern onto tracing paper. Number the pieces to indicate the stitching order. Using fabric pieces that are larger than the numbered areas, place fabrics for #1 and #2 right sides together. Position paper pattern atop fabrics with printed side of paper facing you *(Photo A)*. Make sure the fabric for #1 is under that area and that edges of fabrics extend ¼" beyond stitching line between the two sections.

2. Using a short machine stitch so papers will tear off easily later, stitch on line between the two areas, extending stitching into seam allowances at ends of seams.

3. Open out pieces and press or finger press the seam *(Photo B)*. The right sides of the fabric pieces will be facing out on the back side of the paper pattern.

4. Flip the work over and fold back paper pattern on stitched line. Trim seam allowance to ¼", being careful not to cut paper pattern *(Photo C)*.

5. Continue to add pieces in numerical order until pattern is covered. Use rotary cutter and ruler to trim excess paper and fabric along outer pattern lines *(Photos D and E)*.

6. Carefully tear off foundation paper after blocks are joined.

Baby Rose Crib Set

Welcome a new arrival with more than just a crib quilt. Use coordinating fabrics to create matching bumper pads, dust ruffle, and crib sheet. You'll save a lot by making your own, and you can spend the extra dollars on fabric for your next quilt!

NINE PATCH QUILT

PROJECT RATING: EASY

Size: 38⅛" × 44½"

Blocks: 42 (4½") Nine Patch blocks

MATERIALS

12 fat quarters★★ assorted medium pink, yellow, blue, and green prints if making both quilt and bumper pads **OR** 12 fat eighths★ for quilt only

⅝ yard cream print for strip sets

⅝ yard light pink print for setting squares

⅞ yard medium pink print for setting triangles and binding

1½ yards backing fabric

Crib-size quilt batting

★fat eighth = 9" × 20"

★★fat quarter = 18" × 20"

NOTE: Fabrics in the items shown are from the Seaside Rose collection by 3 Sisters for Moda.

Cutting

Measurements include ¼" seam allowances.

From each fat quarter (or fat eighth), cut:

• 2 (2" × 20") strips for strip sets as shown in *Fat Quarter Cutting Diagram.*

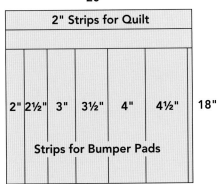

2" Strips for Quilt

2" 2½" 3" 3½" 4" 4½" | 18"

Strips for Bumper Pads

20"

Fat Quarter Cutting Diagram

From cream print, cut:

• 10 (2"-wide) strips. Cut strips in half to make 20 (2" × 20") strips for strip sets.

From light pink print, cut:

• 4 (5"-wide) strips. From strips, cut 30 (5") setting squares.

From medium pink print, cut:

• 2 (7⅝"-wide) strips. From strips, cut 6 (7⅝") squares and 2 (4") squares. Cut 7⅝" squares in half diagonally in both directions to make 24 side setting triangles (2 are extra). Cut 4" squares in half diagonally to make 4 corner setting triangles.

• 5 (2¼"-wide) strips for binding.

Block Assembly

1. Join 2 cream print strips and 1 medium print strip as shown in *Light Strip Set Diagram.* Make 5 light strip sets. From strip sets, cut 42 (2"-wide) segments.

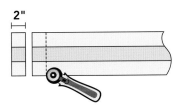

2"

Light Strip Set Diagram

2. Join 2 medium print strips and 1 cream print strip as shown in *Medium Strip Set Diagram.* Make 9 medium strip sets. From strip sets, cut 84 (2"-wide) segments.

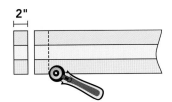

2"

Medium Strip Set Diagram

3. Join 2 medium segments and 1 light segment as shown in *Nine Patch Block Diagrams.* Make 42 Nine Patch blocks.

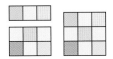

Nine Patch Block Diagrams

Quilt Assembly

1. Lay out blocks, setting squares, and setting triangles as shown in *Quilt Top Assembly Diagram* on page 80.

2. Join into diagonal rows; join rows to complete quilt top.

Finishing

1. Layer backing, batting, and quilt top; baste. Quilt as desired. Quilt shown was quilted with a square grid.

2. Join 2¼"-wide pink print strips into 1 continuous piece for straight-grain French-fold binding. Add binding to quilt.

BUMPER PADS

MATERIALS

Pieces remaining from fat quarters for quilt **OR** 12 fat quarters★★ assorted medium pink, yellow, blue, and green prints

1⅛ yards pink print for ties

1⅝ yards pink-and-white print backing fabric

1 set poly-fil bumper pads

★★fat quarter = 18" × 20"

Cutting

Measurements include ¼" seam allowances for patchwork and ⅜" seam allowances for outer seams.

Quilt Top Assembly Diagram

NOTE: If making both quilt and bumper pads, refer to *Fat Quarter Cutting Diagram* on page 79, and cut 2"-wide crosswise strips for quilt before cutting lengthwise strips for bumper pad strip sets.

From remaining piece of each fat quarter, cut:

• 1 strip in each of the following widths: 2", 2½", 3", 3½", 4", and 4½" as shown in *Fat Quarter Cutting Diagram* on page 79.

From pink print, cut:

• 12 (3"-wide) strips. From strips, cut 24 (3" × 20") rectangles for ties.

From pink-and-white print, cut:

• 2 (27"-wide) strips. From strips, cut 6 (11¾" × 27") backing pieces.

Bumper Pad Assembly

1. Join random-width medium print strips to make a strip set at least 27" wide as shown in *Strip Set Diagram*. Make 6 strip sets.

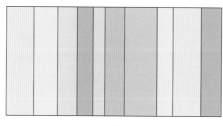

Strip Set Diagram

2. Press tie rectangle in half lengthwise, wrong sides facing, to create center fold. Open out tie and press both edges so they meet on the wrong side of center fold. Press tie in half again, concealing raw edges in fold. Turn

under ¼" on each end. Machine top-stitch ends and long edge of tie. Make 24 ties.

3. Referring to *Bumper Pad Assembly Diagram,* lay backing rectangle atop strip set, right sides together. Using a ⅜" seam, stitch **long** edges of bumper pad cover, leaving a 10" opening on one side for turning.

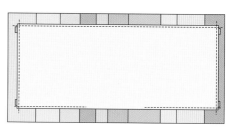

Bumper Pad Assembly Diagram

4. Fold tie strip in half and line up fold with short edge of backing rectangle so it will be caught in seam. Tie should be right next to seam on long side. Repeat for remaining corners. Using a ⅜" seam, stitch short edges of bumper pad, catching ties in seam.

5. Trim strip set even with backing fabric. Turn bumper pad cover right side out through opening, using ties to pull corners out *(Bumper Pad Diagram)*. Roll up 1 foam strip, insert and unroll in bumper pad cover, and hand stitch opening closed. Make 6 bumper pads.

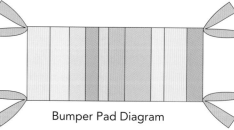

Bumper Pad Diagram

Sew Smart™

To make the bumper pads even softer, cut pieces of poly-fil® Bumper Batting the same size as bumper pads and insert into bumper pad cover.

CRIB SHEET

MATERIALS

2 yards pink-and-white print
1½ yards (¼"-wide) elastic

Cutting

From pink-and-white print, cut:
• 1 (42" × 67") rectangle for sheet.

Crib Sheet Assembly

1. Referring to *Crib Sheet Diagram*, cut a 7" square from each corner of crib sheet. Mark a dot 12½" from corner on long edge of sheet. Mark another dot ½" from first dot. Repeat for remaining corners.
2. Referring to *Corner Stitching Diagrams*, pin sides A and B together, right sides facing. Stitch with ¼" seam. Serge seam allowances or finish with a zigzag stitch. Repeat for remaining corners.

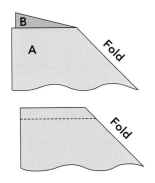

Corner Stitching Diagrams

3. Press under ¼" on raw edges of sheet. Press under ½" to form casing. Machine stitch around casing, leaving ½" spaces between dots open to insert elastic.
4. Cut 2 (27"-long) elastic pieces. Insert 1 piece of elastic in casing and run elastic around short end of sheet. Secure ends of elastic at dots. Stitch openings closed. Repeat for opposite end of sheet.

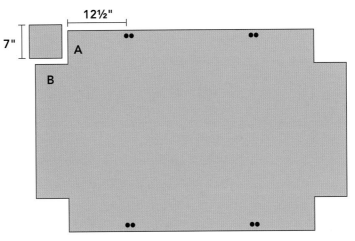

12½"

7"

A

B

Crib Sheet Diagram

DUST RUFFLE

MATERIALS

4 yards floral print

Cutting

Measurements include ½" seam allowances.
From floral print, cut:
• 1 (27" × 52") base rectangle.
• 3 (13" × 84") **lengthwise** strips. From strips, cut 2 (13" × 80") side ruffles and 2 (13" × 42") end ruffles.

Dust Ruffle Assembly

1. Press under ½" on both short sides and 1 long side of side ruffle. Press under again to form a double hem. Machine topstitch hem. Repeat for remaining 3 ruffles.
2. Gather unhemmed edge of side ruffle until it measures the same length as long side of base rectangle. Place side ruffle atop base rectangle, right sides together and raw edges even. Stitch with ½" seam. Zigzag stitch or serge raw edges if desired. Repeat for other side ruffle.

3. Gather unhemmed edge of end ruffle until it measures the same length as short side of base rectangle. Place side ruffle atop base rectangle, right sides together and raw edges even. Stitch with ½" seam. Zigzag stitch or serge raw edges if desired. Repeat for other end ruffle. ✳

Diaper Bag

Six outer pockets keep baby's things well organized in this roomy tote.

PROJECT RATING: EASY
Size: 16" × 12½" × 4"

MATERIALS

1¼ yards double-sided prequilted
  fabric
Size 16/100 Denim or Sharp
  sewing machine needles
Optional: Walking foot or
  even-feed presser foot

Cutting

Open out fabric to single thickness and cut pieces as indicated in *Cutting Diagram*. Cut a 1½" × 7" rectangle from fabric scraps for button loop closure. Remove quilting stitches and use a single layer of fabric for loop.

Bag Assembly

1. Fold button loop strip in half lengthwise; press. Fold raw edges into center and press. Topstitch along both long edges.

2. Finish top long edge of bag back by double hemming edge, binding edge, or encasing edge with trim strips (see *Sew Easy: Edge Finishes* on page 83). Fold loop in half and catch raw edges in seam of top edge finish. Zigzag or serge side and lower edges of bag back

to clean finish. Repeat for bag front, omitting button loop closure.

3. To define bag sides, fold and press 2" toward wrong side on 1 side of bag front. Starting at top edge, stitch down 6" from top edge close to edge of fold, creating a narrow tuck. Repeat on other side. Repeat to define sides of bag back.

4. With right sides facing, join lower edges of bag front and bag back with a ½" seam. Press seam open. Permanently open and flatten bottom seam by stitching close to edges of seam allowances.

5. Finish long top edge of each pocket by double hemming or binding edge. Zigzag or serge sides and bottom edges of pockets. Press under ½" on long lower edge of each pocket.

6. Pin pocket to right side of bag front up 2" from bottom seam. Topstitch lower edge of pocket to bag front. Baste sides of pocket to sides of bag front. Repeat for bag back.

7. Using diagonal seams, join handle pieces into 1 long piece. Trim handle to 110" long. Join ends to form a loop. Fold handle in half lengthwise with wrong sides facing; press fold to

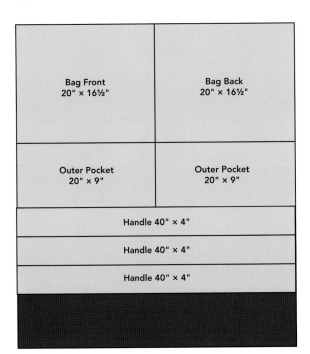

Cutting Diagram

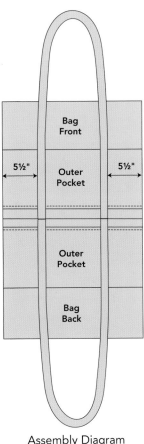

Assembly Diagram

Sew Easy™

Edge Finishes

Double Hemming Edges

Press under ½"; press under again to conceal raw edge. Machine topstitch close to edge to secure hem. For a contrasting hem, fold back side of fabric toward front side, exposing the backing fabric.

Binding Edges

Cut bias or straight-grain binding strips 2¼" wide. Use diagonal seams to join pieces to achieve needed length. Press binding in half with wrong sides facing. Align raw edges of binding with raw edge on wrong side of quilted fabric. Stitch with ¼" seam. Fold binding over raw edge. Machine topstitch folded edge to secure.

Trimmed Edge Finish

Cut trim strip desired width plus 1" for seam allowances (½" on each side). Press under ½" seam allowance on lower edge of trim. Pin right side of trim strip to wrong side of quilted fabric, matching raw edges. Stitch with ½" seam. Bring trim to front and press. Machine topstitch along lower folded edge.

mark handle center. Bring long raw edges into center with wrong sides facing; press. Fold handle in half so raw edges are concealed. Machine topstitch close to long edges of handle and lengthwise down center of handle. Fold handle loop in half and mark divisions with chalk or pins.

8. Referring to *Assembly Diagram*, match handle loop divisions with center bottom seam, and pin handle to bag so outside edges of handles are 5½" from bag sides. Beginning and ending about 2" from bag top, stitch handle to bag, stitching through and dividing each pocket into 3 sections.

9. Stitch sides of bag with French seams or regular ½" seams.

10. With right sides facing, align side seam and center bottom of bag; pin across to create a triangle. Define bag corners by stitching across layers near pocket bottom seams.

Sew Smart™
Sewing French Seams

Place fabric pieces wrong sides together and join with ¼" seam. Fold right side out so right sides of pieces are facing and raw edges of seam allowances are concealed. Stitch with ½" seam that encases and conceals seam allowances. — Liz ✳

Snuggle Quilts

Soft, soft, soft describes these easy-to-make throws you
can quickly assemble to cuddle the little ones you love.

PROJECT RATING: EASY

Size: 44" × 53"

MATERIALS

2½ yards white flannel

3 yards pink or blue print flannel

2¾ yards lavender or yellow print
flannel

Crib-size low-loft batting

Template material

Cutting

Measurements include 1" seam allowances. Instructions are the same for both
quilts. Patterns for Heart and Star are on
page 89. From template material, make
1 cutting line template and 1 stitching line template. Fringe can be cut as
shown on pattern before or after stitching
shape to background square.

From white flannel, cut:

- 10 (8½"-wide) strips. From strips, cut
  40 (8½") A squares.

From pink or blue print flannel, cut:

- 6 (8½"-wide) strips. From strips, cut
  24 (8½") A squares.
- 4 (5¼"-wide) strips. From strips, cut
  28 (5¼") B squares.
- 20 Hearts or Stars.

NOTE: Two layers of rag shapes
are appliquéd to each white fabric
square to give a fuller "bloom" to
the rag shape edges.

**From lavender or yellow print
flannel, cut:**

- 11 (5¼"-wide) strips. From strips, cut
  72 (5¼") B squares.
- 20 Hearts or Stars.

From batting, cut:

- 32 (6½") squares.
- 50 (3¼") squares.

Block Assembly

NOTE: Instructions are for pink and
lavender heart snuggle quilt. For
star quilt, substitute blue and yellow
prints for pink and lavender prints
and stars for hearts.

1. Center 1 (6½") batting square between 2 white A squares, right sides
   out. Pin together at corners. Make 20
   white background sandwiches. In the
   same manner, make 12 pink print
   background sandwiches.

2. Center 2 matching lavender print
   hearts, both right sides up, atop 1
   white background sandwich. Pin in
   place.

3. Stitch through all layers about ⅝" inside
   edge of hearts as indicated by dotted
   line on pattern. Make 10 lavender
   appliqué blocks. In the same manner,
   use pink hearts to make 10 pink appliqué blocks.

4. Center and trace around heart stitching
   line template on 1 pink background
   sandwich. Stitch through all layers
   on drawn line. Repeat to make 12
   stitched blocks.

5. Center 1 (3¼") batting square between 2 matching lavender print B
   squares, right sides out. Pin together
   at corners. Stitch an X from corner
   to corner through all layers. Make 36
   lavender B blocks. In the same manner,
   make 14 pink B blocks.

Snuggle Quilts

Quilt Assembly

1. Join 2 lavender B blocks, wrong sides facing and using 1" seams as shown in *Corner Unit Diagram*. Make 4 corner units.

Corner Unit Diagram

2. Join 1 pink B block and 2 lavender B blocks as shown in *Setting Unit Diagram*. Make 14 setting units.

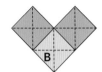

Setting Unit Diagram

3. Lay out appliqué blocks, stitched blocks, setting units, and corner units as shown in *Quilt Top Assembly Diagram*.

4. Place blocks **wrong** sides together and join into diagonal rows using 1" seams. Join rows to complete quilt.

5. Stitch 1" from edge around perimeter of quilt

Quilt Top Assembly Diagram

Sew Smart™

Use a ¼" stack of sticky notes to mark a seam guide on the bed of your sewing machine. Measure 1" from the needle and press stack of notes in place to use as a guide for sewing a 1" seam allowance.
—Marianne

Finishing

1. Snip seam allowances of squares and hearts approximately every ¼".

2. Machine wash and dry quilt to make the fringe "bloom."

Sew Smart™

Wash and dry quilt at a laundromat unless your washer has a lint screen that can be cleaned. Clean out dryer lint screen about every 10 minutes during the drying cycle. —Liz

DESIGNER

Kay Gentry started sewing when she was eight, and has never stopped. For the past nineteen years, she has concentrated on quilting, learning different techniques and timesaving shortcuts. Kay and her husband live in Beavercreek, Ohio, where she teaches quilting and designs patterns for AccuQuilt®. You may contact her at her pattern company: www.nobleneedle.com ✳

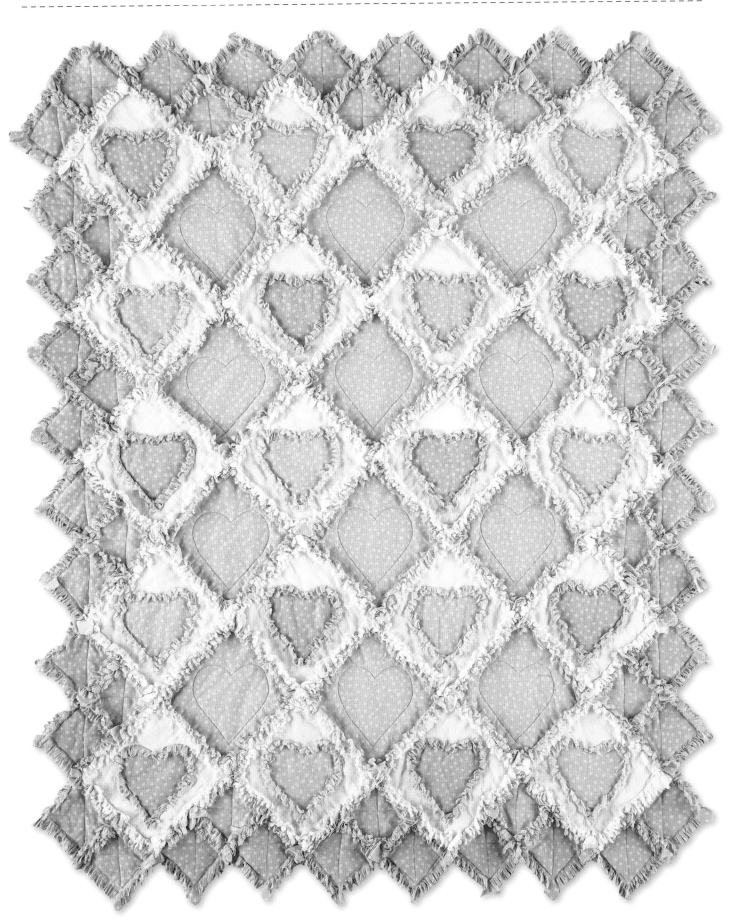

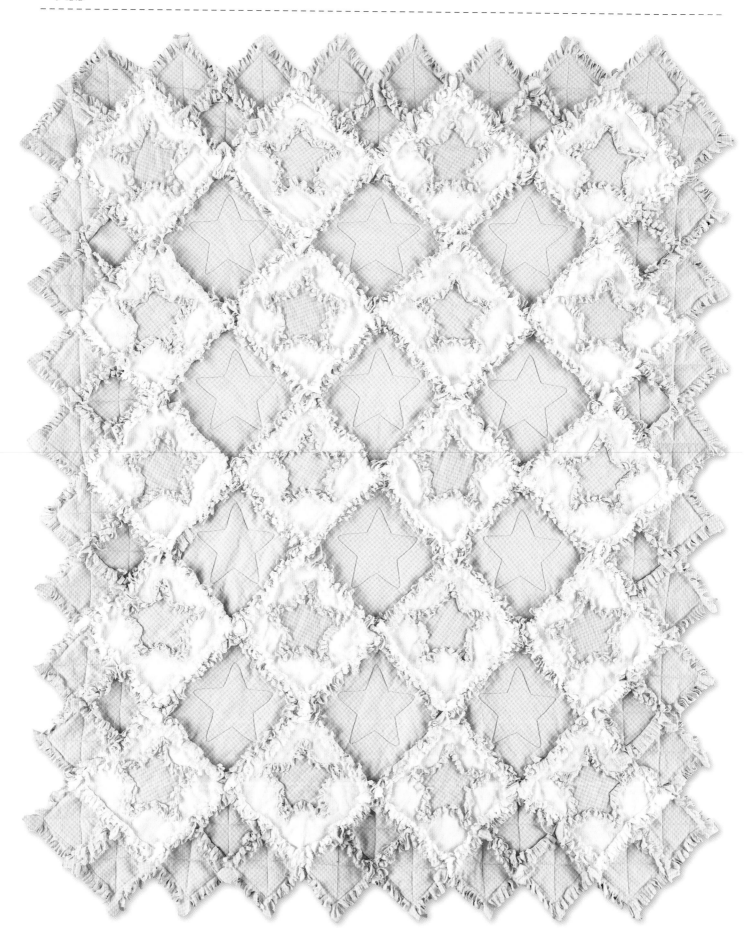

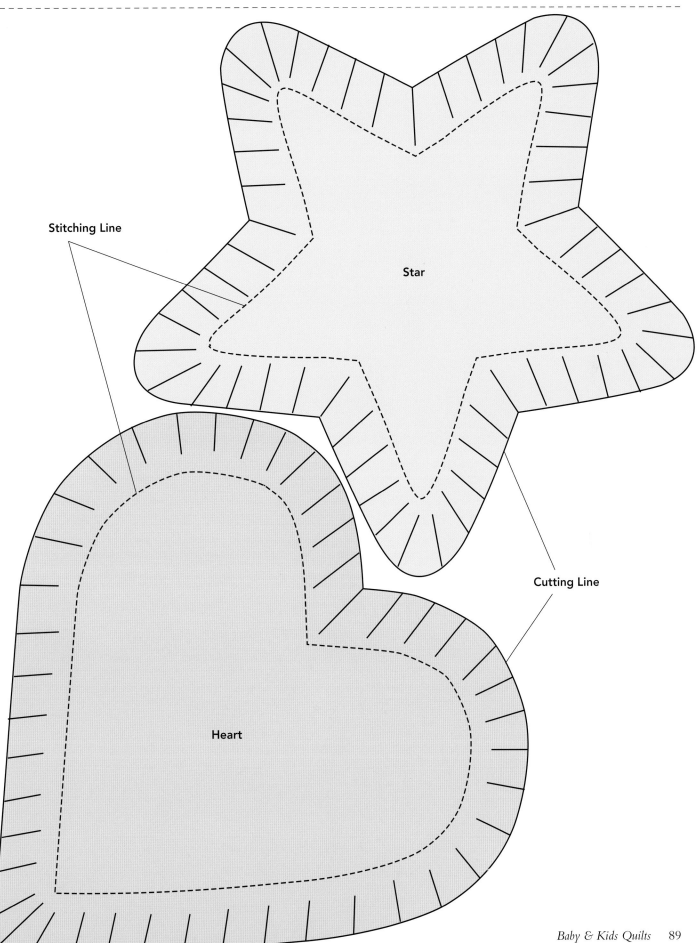

Stitching Line

Star

Cutting Line

Heart

Teague's Turtles

Piece these adorable turtles on paper foundations. It's fun!

PROJECT RATING: INTERMEDIATE
Size: 50" × 50"
Blocks: 9 (12") Turtle blocks

MATERIALS

18 fat quarters★★ assorted bright prints
⅝ yard black-and-white check
1 fat eighth★ green print
1 fat eighth★ red print
1⅛ yards animal border print
½ yard green plaid for binding
9 scraps with dots from ¼"–½" diameter for eyes
Paper for foundations
3¼ yards backing fabric
Twin-size quilt batting
★fat eighth = 9" × 20"
★★fat quarters = 18" × 20"

Cutting

Patterns for foundation piecing are on page 94. Measurements include ¼" seam allowances. Border strips are exact length needed. You may want to make them longer to allow for piecing variations.

NOTE: For instructions on paper foundation piecing, see *Sew Easy: Paper Foundation Piecing* on page 77, or visit www.FonsandPorter.com/sepfp.

From each of 9 fat quarters, cut:
• 1 E.
• 1 F.
• 1 H.
Remaining fabric will be used for background pieces (A2, A3, B2, B3, B4, C2, C3, C4, D2, D3, G2, G3, G4) when foundation piecing.

From each remaining fat quarter, cut:
• 1 Shell.
• 1 (1¾") square for tail.
Remaining fabric will be used for head (A1) and legs (B1, C1, D1, and G1) when foundation piecing.

From black-and-white check, cut:
• 1 (3½"-wide) strip. From strip, cut 4 (3½") I squares.
• 10 (1½"-wide) strips. From 4 strips, cut 2 (1½" × 38½") top and bottom inner borders and 2 (1½" × 36½") side inner borders. Piece remaining strips to make 2 (1½" × 50½") top and bottom outer borders and 2 (1½" × 48½") side outer borders.

From each fat eighth, cut:
• 3 (1½"-wide) strips. From strips, cut 4 (1½" × 5½") K rectangles and 4 (1½" × 3½") J rectangles.

From animal border print, cut:
• 4 (5½"-wide) **lengthwise** strips, centering design in each. From strips, cut 4 (5½" × 38½") borders.

From green plaid, cut:
• 6 (2¼"-wide) strips for binding.

From each dotted scrap, cut:
• 2 circles for eyes.

Block Assembly

1. Trace 9 each of foundation piecing patterns A, B, C, D, and G.

2. Using 1 bright print for shell, 1 bright print for head and legs, and 1 bright print for background, foundation piece one each of sections A, B, C, D, and G in numerical order.

3. Choose 1 (1¾") bright square to match turtle head and legs. Referring to *Tail Unit Diagrams* on page 92, fold square in half, wrong sides facing. Fold top corners down to meet in center as shown. Press.

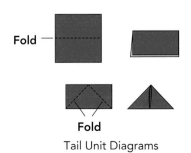

Fold

Fold

Tail Unit Diagrams

4. Referring to *Block Assembly Diagrams*, join sections A, B, C, and D to turtle shell in alphabetical order. Pin tail triangle to shell, raw edges aligned, where indicated on shell pattern. Add pieces E and F, foundation section G, and piece H to complete 1 Turtle block *(Block Diagram)*. Make 9 Turtle blocks.

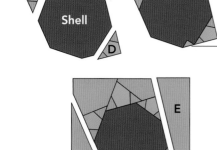

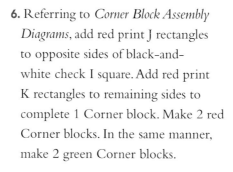

Block Assembly Diagrams

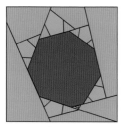

Block Diagram

5. Fuse 2 eyes on each Turtle block. Machine zigzag stitch in place.

6. Referring to *Corner Block Assembly Diagrams*, add red print J rectangles to opposite sides of black-and-white check I square. Add red print K rectangles to remaining sides to complete 1 Corner block. Make 2 red Corner blocks. In the same manner, make 2 green Corner blocks.

Corner Block Assembly Diagrams

Quilt Assembly

1. Lay out Turtle blocks as shown in *Quilt Top Assembly Diagram*. Join into rows; join rows to complete quilt center.

2. Add side inner borders to quilt center. Add top and bottom inner borders to quilt.

3. Add animal print side borders to sides of quilt.

4. Add 1 Corner block to each end of remaining animal print borders to make top and bottom borders. Add borders to quilt.

5. Add side outer borders to quilt center. Add top and bottom outer borders to quilt.

Finishing

1. Divide backing into 2 (1⅜-yard) lengths. Cut 1 piece in half lengthwise to make 2 narrow panels. Join 1 narrow panel to wider panel. Remaining panel is extra and can be used to make a hanging sleeve.

2. Layer backing, batting, and quilt top; baste. Quilt as desired. Quilt shown was quilted with assorted filler designs on the turtle shells, meandering in the background, and flowers in the borders *(Quilting Diagram)*.

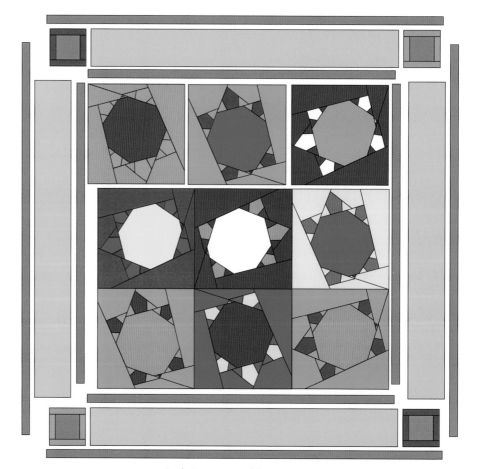

Quilt Top Assembly Diagram

3. Join 2¼"-wide green plaid strips into 1 continuous piece for straight-grain French-fold binding. Add binding to quilt.

Quilting Diagram

DESIGNER

As a teenager, Rachel Wells' first attempt at tying a quilt discouraged her from even thinking about quiltmaking! Fortunately, about 20 years later, she tried quilting again and is now overflowing with excitement and inspiration! Rachel loves learning new techniques and playing wih color and texture. ✳

TRIED & TRUE

Bali Batiks are perfect for turtles! The green and blue print mimics the texture of a shell.

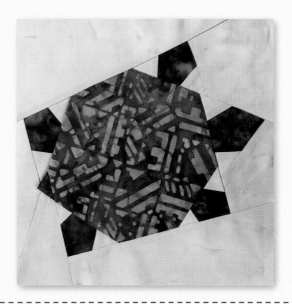

Teague's Turtles

Enlarge Designs 200%

Permisssion is granted by *Love of Quilting* to enlarge patterns to correct size using photocopy machine.

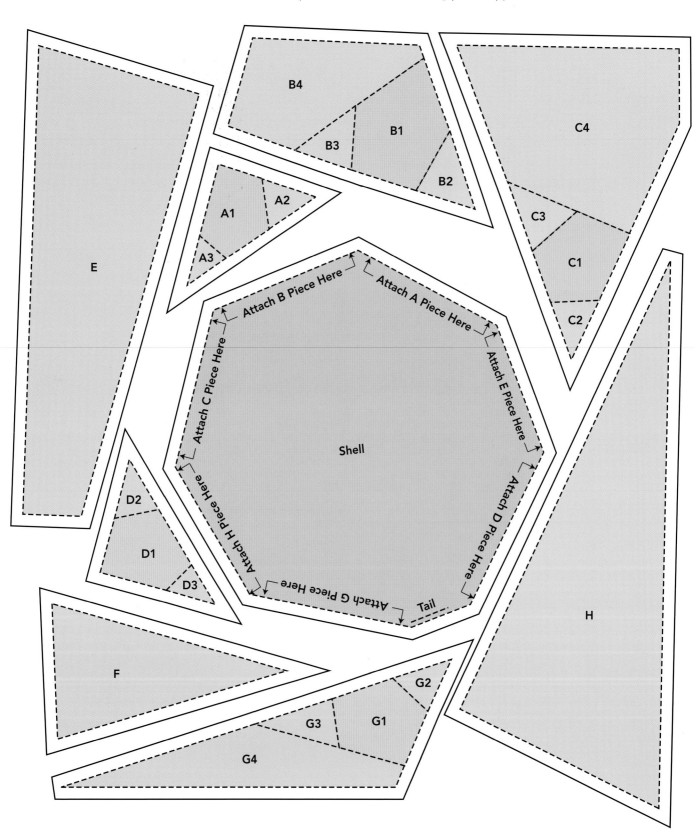

Pillowcase

Create a fun pillowcase to match the quilt you give. Or, visit your stash and use up some of the great theme fabrics you've collected.

PROJECT RATING: EASY
Size: 19" × 30"
(Fits a standard bed pillow)

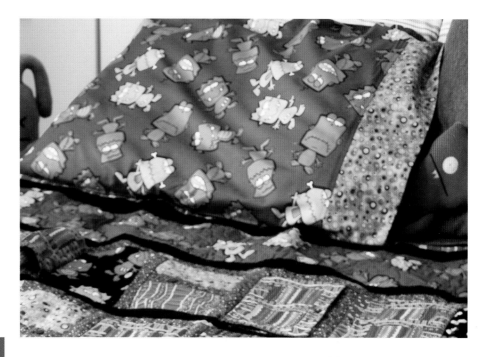

MATERIALS

¾ yard novelty or theme fabric for pillowcase
¼ yard contrasting fabric for band
2"-wide strip accent fabric (optional)

Cutting

From novelty fabric, cut:
- 1 (27" × 40") rectangle.

From contrasting fabric, cut:
- 1 (9" × 40") strip.

From accent fabric, cut:
- 1 (2" × 40") strip.

Assembly

1. Referring to *Diagram 1*, fold pillowcase fabric into a 20" × 27" rectangle with right sides facing. Stitch along top and side edge with ½" seam. Turn pillowcase right side out.

Diagram 1

Diagram 2

Diagram 3

2. With right sides facing, join short ends of band strip with a ½" seam. Press under ½" along 1 long edge of band.

3. Join short ends of accent strip with a ½" seam. Fold accent strip in half with wrong sides facing; press.

> ## Sew **Smart**™
> Zigzag, pink, or serge raw edges of seams to help prevent raveling during washing. —Liz

4. Pin accent strip to right side of pillowcase, aligning raw edges. Pin contrasting band atop accent strip as shown in *Diagram 2*. Stitch around pillowcase through all layers with a ½" seam. Press seam allowance toward pillowcase.

5. Turn band to inside of pillowcase, aligning fold of band with seam. Press. Stitch in the ditch through all layers (*Diagram 3*). ✳

Flower Power

Layered fusible appliqué makes this whimsical young girl's quilt easy to stitch and assemble. Make one for your little princess.

PROJECT RATING: INTERMEDIATE

Size: 64" × 84"

Blocks: 35 (8") blocks

MATERIALS

2¼ yards pink floral print for border and binding

2¼ yards light pink print for block backgrounds

12 fat quarters★★ assorted pink, blue, green, and yellow prints for flowers

1 fat eighth★ bright yellow solid for flower centers

1⅝ yards blue print for sashing

⅜ yard pink print for sashing squares

5 yards backing fabric

Twin-size quilt batting

Paper-backed fusible web

★fat eighth = 9" × 20"

★★fat quarter = 18" × 20"

NOTE: Fabrics in the quilt shown are from the Zoe collection by Max & Nobie for Moda.

Cutting

Measurements include ¼" seam allowances. Patterns for appliqué are on page 100. Follow manufacturer's instructions for using fusible web. Border strips are exact length needed. You may want to make them longer to allow for piecing variations.

From pink floral print, cut:

• 8 (6½"-wide) strips. Piece strips to make 2 (6½" × 72½") side borders and 2 (6½" × 64½") top and bottom borders.

• 8 (2¼"-wide) strips for binding.

From light pink print, cut:

• 9 (8½"-wide) strips. From strips, cut 35 (8½") squares.

From each fat quarter, cut:

• 3 Outer Flowers.

• 3 Inner Flowers.

From bright yellow fat eighth, cut:

• 35 Centers.

From blue print, cut:

• 6 (8½"-wide) strips. From strips, cut 82 (8½" × 2½") sashing strips.

From pink print, cut:

• 3 (2½"-wide) strips. From strips, cut 48 (2½") sashing squares.

Block Assembly

1. Referring to *Sew Easy: Unit Method for Appliqué* on page 101, assemble 1 Outer Flower, 1 Inner Flower, and 1 Center.

2. Center 1 Flower Unit on light pink background square as shown in *Block Diagram*.

Block Diagram

3. Fuse pieces in place. Machine zigzag edges of appliqué using matching thread. Make 35 blocks.

Quilt Assembly

1. Lay out blocks, sashing strips, and sashing squares as shown in *Quilt Top Assembly Diagram* on page 98. Join into rows; join rows to complete quilt center.

2. Add pink floral print side borders to quilt center. Add top and bottom borders to quilt.

Finishing

1. Divide backing fabric into 2 (2½-yard) lengths. Cut 1 piece in half lengthwise to make 2 narrow panels. Join 1 narrow panel to each side of wider panel; press seam allowances toward narrow panels.

2. Layer backing, batting, and quilt top; baste. Quilt as desired. Quilt shown was outline quilted around each flower unit, quilted in the ditch around sashing, and has parallel lines in border *(Quilting Diagram)*.

3. Join 2¼"-wide pink floral print strips into 1 continuous piece for straight-grain French-fold binding. Add binding to quilt.

Quilting Diagram

Quilt Top Assembly Diagram

TRIED & TRUE

Fabrics shown in our version of this antique-inspired design are from the Pennsylvania Bluestone collection by Deborah Hearn for Windham Fabrics.

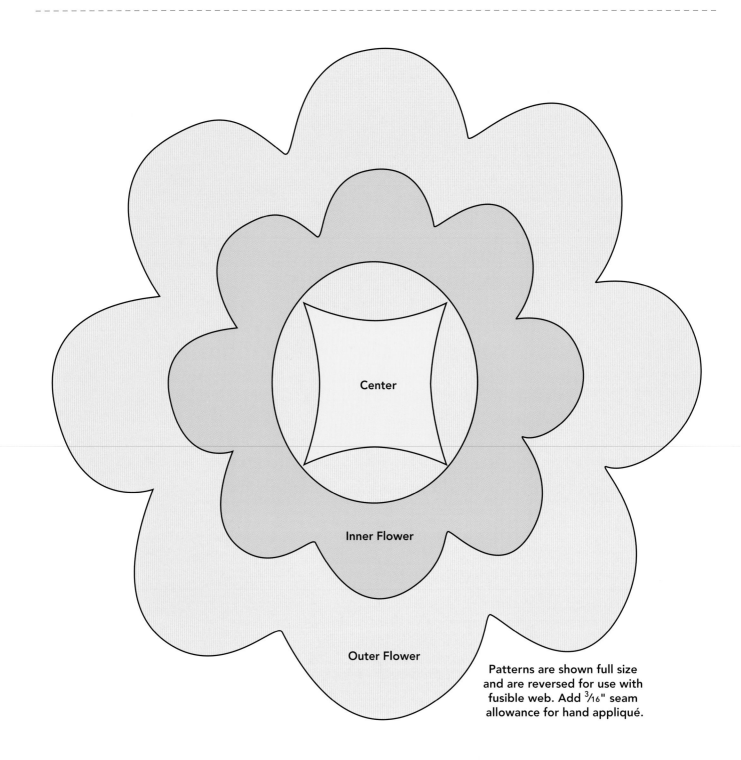

Center

Inner Flower

Outer Flower

Patterns are shown full size
and are reversed for use with
fusible web. Add ³⁄₁₆" seam
allowance for hand appliqué.

"I saw this flower appliqué on an antique quilt
and thought it would be fun to make a modern
version for my daughter" —Jean Nolte *

Sew Easy™

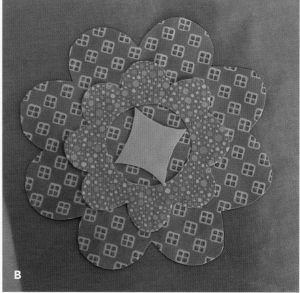

Unit Method for Appliqué

When making appliqué blocks that will be machine stitched, use this method
to assemble and stitch some pieces before fusing them to the background.
Work on a see-through appliqué pressing sheet when assembling the pieces so
you don't get fusible residue on your ironing surface.

1. Trace appliqué shapes on paper side of fusible web. For large pieces, window the fusible web by cutting ¼" inside drawn line. Press fusible web on wrong side of appliqué fabric *(Photo A)*.
2. Cut out appliqué pieces on drawn line. Remove paper backing from all appliqué pieces.
3. Working from background to foreground, layer appliqué pieces on pressing sheet *(Photo B)*.
4. Fuse in place. Peel assembled units from pressing sheet.
5. Machine stitch around smaller inner shapes.
6. Position stitched units atop background and stitch around outside edges.

Sew Smart™
If you don't have a pressing sheet, you can use a piece of the paper backing from fusible web or baker's parchment paper as a substitute. —Marianne

Pinwheel Pastels

Designer Michele Scott chose candy colors and soft pastels to make her Pinwheel blocks. The twisted setting makes them appear to be spinning.

PROJECT RATING: INTERMEDIATE
Size: 55" × 64"
Blocks: 30 (9") blocks

MATERIALS

9 fat quarters★ assorted medium prints in green, yellow, blue, lavender, pink, and orange
⅜ yard each of 10 assorted light prints in green, yellow, blue, lavender, pink, and orange
1 yard purple print for inner border and binding
1 yard multicolor print for outer border
3½ yards backing fabric
Twin-size quilt batting
★fat quarter = 18" × 20"

NOTE: Fabrics in the quilt shown are from the Nature's Palette Candy Tones and Soft Pastel collections by Michele Scott for Lyndhurst Studio.

Cutting

Measurements include ¼" seam allowances. Border strips are exact length needed. You may want to make them longer to allow for piecing variations. Pattern for B triangle is on page 105.

From each medium print fat quarter, cut:
• 2 (4¾"-wide) strips. From strips, cut 6 (4¾") squares. Cut squares in half diagonally to make 12 half-square A triangles.

From each light print, cut:
• 1 (4¾"-wide) strip. From strip, cut 6 (4¾") squares. Cut squares in half diagonally to make 12 half-square A triangles.

From remainder of each of 5 light prints, cut:
• 12 B triangles.

From remainder of each of 5 light prints, cut:
• 12 B triangles reversed.

From purple print, cut:
• 1 (4¾"-wide) strip. From strip, cut 6 (4¾") squares. Cut squares in half diagonally to make 12 half-square A triangles.

• 7 (2¼"-wide) strips for binding.
• 6 (1½"-wide) strips. Piece strips to make 2 (1½" × 54½") side inner borders and 2 (1½" × 47½") top and bottom inner borders.

From multicolor print, cut:
• 6 (4½"-wide) strips. Piece strips to make 2 (4½" × 56½") side outer borders and 2 (4½" × 55½") top and bottom outer borders.

Block Assembly

1. Choose 1 set of 4 matching medium print A triangles and 4 matching light print A triangles. Join 1 medium print triangle and 1 light print triangle as shown in *Triangle-Square Diagrams*. Make 30 sets of 4 matching triangle-squares.

Triangle-Square Diagrams

2. Lay out 1 set of 4 triangle-squares as shown in *Pinwheel Unit Diagrams*. Join into rows; join rows to make 1 Pinwheel Unit. Make 30 Pinwheel Units.

Pinwheel Unit Diagrams

3. Add B triangles to Pinwheel Unit as shown in *Block Assembly Diagram* to make 1 left-tilting block *(Block Diagrams)*. Make 15 left-tilting blocks.

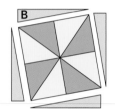

Block Assembly Diagram

Block Diagrams

4. In the same manner, make 15 right-tilting blocks using remaining Pinwheel Units and B triangles reversed.

Quilt Assembly

1. Lay out blocks as shown in *Quilt Top Assembly Diagram*. Join blocks into rows; join rows to complete quilt center.
2. Add purple print side inner borders to quilt center. Add top and bottom inner borders to quilt.
3. Repeat for outer borders.

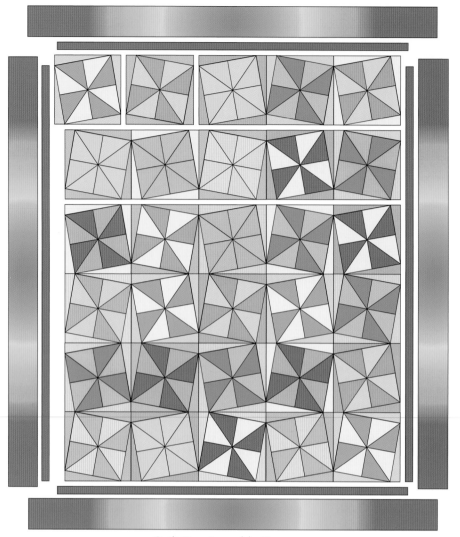

Quilt Top Assembly Diagram

Finishing

1. Divide backing into 2 (1¾-yard) lengths. Join panels lengthwise. Seam will run horizontally.
2. Layer backing, batting, and quilt top; baste. Quilt as desired. Quilt shown was quilted with an allover design *(Quilting Diagram)*.
3. Join 2¼"-wide purple print strips into 1 continuous piece for straight-grain French-fold binding. Add binding to quilt.

Quilting Diagram

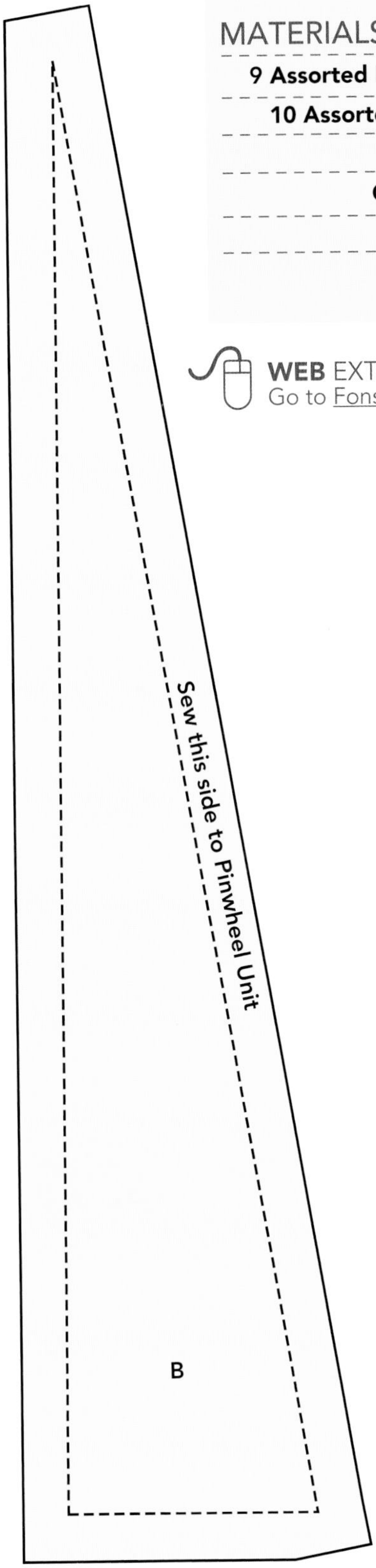

SIZE OPTIONS

	Crib (37" × 55")	Twin (64" × 91")	Full (82" × 91")
Blocks	15	54	72
Setting	3 × 5	6 × 9	8 × 9

MATERIALS

	Crib (37" × 55")	Twin (64" × 91")	Full (82" × 91")
9 Assorted Medium Prints	½ yard each	1 yard each	1¼ yards each
10 Assorted Light Prints	⅝ yard each	1⅜ yards each	1⅝ yards each
Purple Print	¼ yard	1¼ yards	1½ yards
Gradated Print	¼ yard	1¼ yards	1⅝ yards
Backing Fabric	1¾ yards	5½ yards	7½ yards
Batting	Crib-size	Full-size	Queen-size

 WEB EXTRA
Go to FonsandPorter.com/ppastelsizes to download *Quilt Top Assembly Diagrams* for these size options.

Sew this side to Pinwheel Unit

B

TRIED & TRUE

We mixed bold colors and black prints from the Paulina collection by P&B Textiles.

DESIGNER

Michele Scott is an award-winning quilt artist who teaches, lectures, and designs. She especially enjoys machine work and embellishing.

Contact her at:

michele@piecefulquilter.com

www.piecefulquilter.com ❊

Playful Pups

Stitch twelve scrappy patchwork pups to delight a child.
Reproduction 1930s prints are perfect for cottage style décor.

PROJECT RATING: INTERMEDIATE
Size: 42" × 55½"
Blocks: 12 (12") Dog blocks

MATERIALS

20 fat eighths★ 1930s reproduction
  prints
1¾ yards cream solid for
  background
½ yard green print for binding
2¾ yards backing fabric
Crib-size quilt batting
★fat eighth = 9" × 20"

Cutting

Measurements include ¼" seam allowances.

From each fat eighth, cut:

• 3 (2"-wide) strips. From 12 strips, cut
72 (2") B squares. Remaining strips
are for strip sets.

**From remaining pieces of fat eighths,
cut a total of:**

• 3 (2¾") squares. Cut squares in half
diagonally in both directions to make
12 quarter-square D triangles.

> ### Sew **Smart**™
>
> For more variety, cut a few
> extra 2¾" squares. Cut the
> squares into quarter-square D
> triangles. You will have some
> triangles left over. —Marianne

• 18 (2⅜") squares. Cut squares in half
diagonally to make 36 half-square E
triangles.

From cream solid, cut:

• 4 (3½"-wide) strips. From strips, cut
12 (3½" × 6½") A rectangles and
12 (3½" × 5") G rectangles.

• 1 (2¾"-wide) strip. From strip, cut
3 (2¾") squares. Cut squares in half
diagonally in both directions to make
12 quarter-square D triangles.

• 1 (2⅜"-wide) strip. From strip, cut
12 (2⅜") squares. Cut squares in half
diagonally to make 24 half-square E
triangles.

• 17 (2"-wide) strips. From strips, cut
24 (2" × 12½") I rectangles,
24 (2" × 9½") H rectangles, and
24 (2" × 3½") C rectangles.

From green print, cut:

• 6 (2¼"-wide) strips for binding.

Block Assembly

1. Join 4 (2"-wide) print strips as shown
in *Strip Set Diagram*. Make 12 strip
sets. From strips sets, cut 103 (2"-wide)
segments.

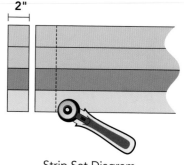

2"

Strip Set Diagram

2. Join 3 strip set segments as shown in
Body Unit Diagrams. Make 12 Body
Units.

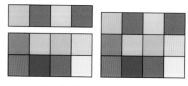

Body Unit Diagrams

3. Referring to *Unit 1 Diagrams*, place 1
print B square atop 1 cream A rectangle,
right sides facing. Stitch diagonally
from corner to corner as shown. Trim
¼" beyond stitching. Press open to

reveal triangle. Repeat for adjacent corner to complete 1 Unit 1. Make 12 Unit 1.

Unit 1 Diagrams

4. In the same manner, join 1 print B square to 1 cream C rectangle as shown in *Unit 2 Diagrams*. Make 12 Unit 2.

Unit 2 Diagrams

5. Referring to *Unit 3 Diagrams*, join 1 print D triangle, 1 cream D triangle, and 1 print E triangle to complete 1 Unit 3. Make 12 Unit 3.

Unit 3 Diagrams

6. Join 1 print E triangle and 1 cream E triangle as shown in *Triangle-Square Diagrams*. Make 24 triangle-squares.

Triangle-Square Diagrams

7. Lay out 2 triangle-squares, 1 Unit 2, 1 Unit 3, and 1 print B square to as shown in *Head Unit Assembly Diagram*. Join into rows; join rows to complete 1 Head Unit *(Head Unit Diagram)*. Make 12 Head Units.

 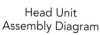

Head Unit Assembly Diagram   Head Unit Diagram

8. Join 2 print B squares and 1 cream C rectangle as shown in *Unit 4 Diagrams*. Make 12 Unit 4.

Unit 4 Diagrams

9. Referring to *Block Assembly Diagram*, lay out Unit 1, 1 Body Unit, 1 Unit 4, 1 Head Unit, and 1 cream G rectangle. Join to make Dog Unit.

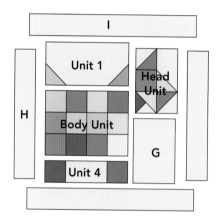

Block Assembly Diagram

10. Add 1 H rectangle to each side of Dog Unit. Add I rectangles to top and bottom of Dog Unit to complete 1 Dog block *(Block Diagram)*. Make 12 Dog blocks.

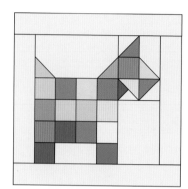

Block Diagram

Quilt Assembly

1. Referring to *Quilt Top Assembly Diagram*, join 2 strip set segments to make 1 vertical sashing unit. Make 16 vertical sashing units. In the same

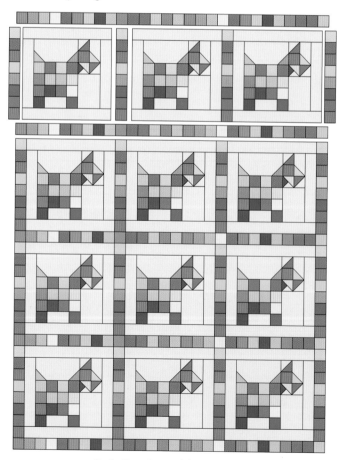

Quilt Top Assembly Diagram

make 1 vertical sashing unit. Make 16 vertical sashing units. In the same manner, join 7 segments to make 1 horizontal sashing unit. Make 5 horizontal sashing units.

2. Lay out blocks and sashing units as shown in *Quilt Top Assembly Diagram*.

3. Join into rows; join rows to complete quilt top.

Finishing

1. Divide backing into 2 (1⅜-yard) lengths. Cut 1 piece in half length-wise to make 2 narrow panels. Join 1 narrow panel to wider panel; press seam allowances toward narrow panel. Seam will run horizontally. Remaining panel is extra and can be used to make a hanging sleeve.

2. Layer backing, batting, and quilt top; baste. Quilt as desired. Quilt shown was quilted in the ditch around print squares and triangles and has diagonal crosshatching in background.

3. Join 2¼"-wide green print strips into 1 continuous piece for straight-grain French-fold binding. Add binding to quilt.

TRIED & TRUE

For a cute wallhanging, use just one print for the dog. Instead of piecing the body, cut 1 (5" × 6½") rectangle. For a bow, cut 1 (2" × 9") strip. Fold strip in half length-wise, and stitch ¼" from raw edges, leaving an opening on the long side for turning. Turn right side out, press, and whipstitch opening closed. Tie into a bow and attach to dog's neck. ✳

Quillows for Kids

These great gifts are a one-afternoon or evening project. Make one for a kid who loves to cuddle up and read.

PROJECT RATING: EASY

Size: 39½" × 65"

MATERIALS

2 yards blue print for quillow back

2 yards novelty print for quillow front

2 pre-printed panels (18" square) **OR** 2 fat quarters★ coordinating print for pocket

Twin-size quilt batting **OR** 2 yards flannel or fleece.
(If you use flannel or fleece, you will need an 18" square of batting for pocket.)

Sewing machine with walking foot

★fat quarter = 18" × 20"

Cutting

Measurements include ¼" seam allowances.

From blue print, cut:

• 1 (40" × 65½") rectangle for quillow back.

From novelty print, cut:

• 1 (42" × 68") rectangle for quillow front.

From each pre-printed panel (OR fat quarter), cut:

• 1 (18") square for pocket.

From batting (OR flannel or fleece), cut:

• 1 (43" × 69") rectangle.

• 1 (18") square.

Quillow Assembly

1. Place 2 pocket squares right sides facing. Place paired squares atop batting square; pin. Stitch around three outer edges, leaving one side open to turn. If pocket has a directional design, leave opening at bottom edge of pocket.

2. Trim corners. Turn pocket right side out. Quilt, if desired.

3. With right sides facing, center pocket along bottom edge of quillow back piece, aligning raw edges as shown in *Quillow Asembly Diagrams*. Machine baste in place.

NOTE: The side of the pocket that is placed facing the quillow back will become the front of the pillow when the quillow is folded.

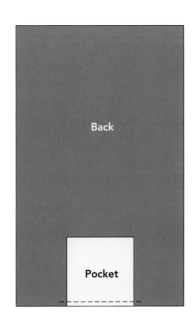
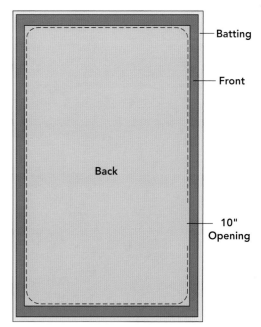

Quillow Assembly Diagrams

4. Place quillow front atop batting rectangle, right side up; place quillow back atop quillow front, right sides facing. Use a plate or other round object as a guide to mark rounded corners. Pin; stitch around outer edges, rounding corners. Leave a 10" opening on one side for turning.

Sew Smart™

Before stitching, put a 10"-long piece of masking tape along the edge of the quillow back where you plan to leave an opening. The tape will remind you not to stitch that section. —Marianne

5. Trim excess fabric. Turn quillow right side out through opening. Whipstitch opening closed.

6. Referring to *Quilting Diagram*, stitch through all layers, stitching pocket down; continue stitching to opposite edge of quillow.

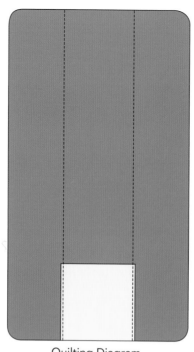

Quilting Diagram

Sew Smart™

A great way to mark the stitching lines for the two lines of quilting that will hold the layers together is to fold and lightly press the quillow fabric, making two lengthwise guidelines. —Liz

Folding Quillow

1. Referring to *Folding Diagrams*, turn the quillow over so the pocket is underneath. Fold lengthwise along quilting lines.

2. Fold the quillow twice as shown.

3. Turn the pocket right side out, tucking the folded quillow into the pocket to make a pillow.

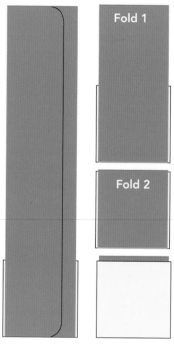

Fold 1

Fold 2

Folding Diagrams

When folded, the quillow turns into a pillow.

SIZE OPTIONS

Use this formula to make a quillow any size you like:

1. Determine the pillow size you want.

2. Cut quillow back width 2" narrower than 3 times the size of the pillow.

3. Cut quillow back length no more than 4 times the size of the pillow.

4. Cut the front slightly larger than the back; cut the batting slightly larger than the front.

Example: For a 10" pillow, cut the back 28" wide (3 × 10" = 30"; 30" − 2" = 28") and 40" long (4 × 10" = 40").

TRIED & TRUE

Fons & Porter staff members made a variety of quillows.

Top: Marianne Fons used a coordinating floral print and stripe in bright colors. **Center:** Liz Porter used a patchwork block for her pocket and chenille for the back of her quillow to make it even more snuggly. **Bottom:** Cindy Hathaway chose a floral panel for the pillow and coordinating prints for the front and back. ✳

Interlocking Windmills

Bright fabrics and unique piecing bring a great new look to the Pinwheel.
You'll want to make more than one!

PROJECT RATING: INTERMEDIATE

Size: 41" × 58½"

MATERIALS

1¼ yards yellow print for background

16 fat eighths★ assorted prints in red, green, orange, and blue

¼ yard orange print for inner border

1 yard dark orange print for outer border

½ yard red print for binding

2¾ yards backing fabric

Fons & Porter Quarter Inch Seam Marker (optional)

Crib-size quilt batting

★fat eighth = 9" × 20"

Cutting

Measurements include ¼" seam allowances. Border strips are exact length needed. You may want to make them longer to allow for piecing variations. Pattern for C triangle is on page 118.

From yellow print, cut:

- 2 (4⅜"-wide) strips. From strips, cut 16 (4⅜") B squares.

NOTE: If NOT using the Fons & Porter Quarter Inch Seam Marker, cut B squares in half diagonally to make half-square triangles.

- 1 (4"-wide) strip. From strip, cut 8 (4") A squares.
- 32 C triangles.

From each assorted print fat eighth, cut:

- 1 (4⅜"-wide) strip. From strip, cut 1 (4⅜") B square.

NOTE: If NOT using the Fons & Porter Quarter Inch Seam Marker, cut B squares in half diagonally to make half-square triangles.

- 2 C triangles.

From orange print, cut:

- 5 (1½"-wide) strips. From strips, cut 2 (1½" × 30½") top and bottom inner borders. Piece remaining strips to make 2 (1½" × 46") side inner borders.

From dark orange print, cut:

- 5 (6"-wide) strips. Piece strips to make 2 (6" × 48") side outer borders and 2 (6" × 41½") top and bottom outer borders.

From red print, cut:

- 6 (2¼"-wide) strips for binding.

Quilt Assembly

1. Make 32 triangle-squares using yellow print and assorted print B squares (*Triangle-Square Diagrams*).

Triangle-Square Diagrams

> ## Sew **Smart**™
>
> See *Sew Easy: Quick Triangle-Squares* on page 119 for instructions to make the triangle-squares using the Fons & Porter Quarter Inch Seam Marker. — Marianne

2. Join 1 yellow print C triangle and 1 assorted print C triangle to make 1 Windmill Blade (*Windmill Blade Diagrams*). Make 32 Windmill Blades.

Windmill Blade Diagrams

3. Lay out Windmill Blades, triangle-squares, and yellow print A squares as shown in *Quilt Top Assembly Diagram*.

> ## Sew **Smart**™
> Take care when laying out Windmill Blades and triangle squares so that all pinwheels spin in the same direction. —Liz

4. Join into vertical rows; join rows to complete quilt center.

5. Add orange print inner borders to sides of quilt. Add inner borders to top and bottom of quilt.

6. Repeat for dark orange print outer borders.

Finishing

1. Divide backing into 2 (1⅜-yard) lengths. Join panels lengthwise. Seam will run horizontally.

2. Layer backing, batting, and quilt top; baste. Quilt as desired. Quilt shown was quilted with curved lines in background and outer border and with loops in inner border (*Quilting Diagram*).

3. Join 2¼"-wide red print strips into 1 continuous piece for straight-grain French-fold binding. Add binding to quilt.

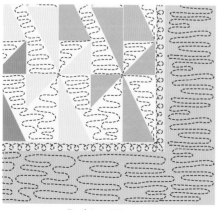

Quilting Diagram

Quilt Top Assembly Diagram

SIZE OPTIONS

Crib (34" × 48") Queen (90" × 100½")

MATERIALS

	Crib (34" × 48")	Queen (90" × 100½")
Yellow Print	¾ yard	4¼ yards
Assorted Prints	9 fat eighths★★	30 fat quarters★
Orange Print	¼ yard	½ yard
Dark Orange Print	¾ yard	2 yards
Red Print	⅜ yard	¾ yard
Backing Fabric	1½ yards	8¼ yards
Batting	Crib-size	King-size

★fat quarter = 18" × 20"

★★fat eighth = 9" × 20"

 WEB EXTRA

Go to www.FonsandPorter.com/windmillsizes to download *Quilt Top Assembly Diagrams* for these size options.

DESIGNERS

Anne Gallo and Susan Raban are well known for their colorful, geometric quilts. They have been working together for thirty years, always focusing on precise machine piecing.

Contact them at: www.YankeeQuilts.com ✳

TRIED & TRUE

Fabrics shown in this version are from the Winter Berries collection by Lydia Quigley for Clothworks.

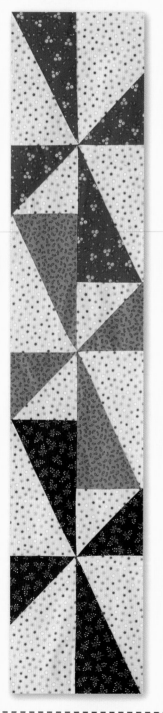

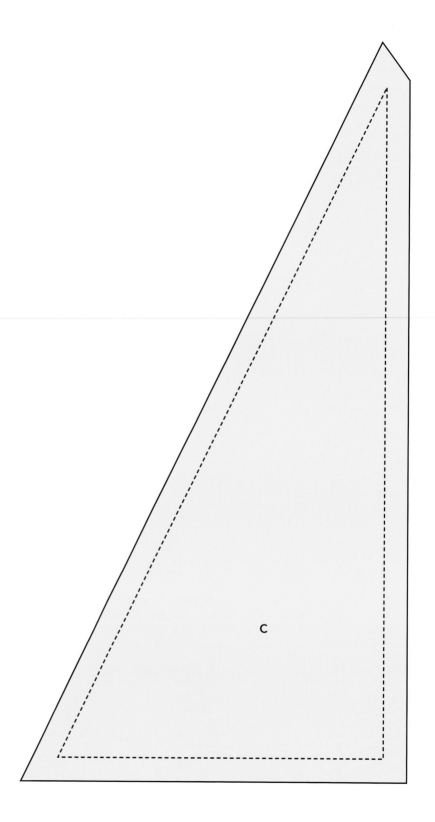

C

Quick Triangle-Squares

Our quick method for making Triangle-Squares
begins with two squares. Use this technique to make the
Triangle-Squares for *Interlocking Windmills* on page 114.
The Fons & Porter Quarter Inch Seam Marker offers a neat
way to mark accurate sewing lines for this method.

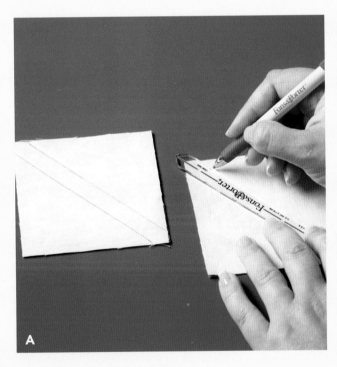

1. From each of 2 fabrics, cut 1 square 7/8" larger than the desired finished size of the triangle-square. For example, to make a triangle-square that will finish 3½" as in the *Interlocking Windmills* quilt on page 114, cut 4⅜" squares.

2. On wrong side of lighter square, place Quarter Inch Seam Marker diagonally across the square, with yellow center line positioned exactly at opposite corners. Mark stitching lines along both sides of Quarter Inch Seam Marker (*Photo A*).

3. Place light square atop darker square, right sides facing; stitch along both marked sewing lines.

4. Cut between rows of stitching to make 2 triangle-squares (*Photo B*).

Hey You!

Kelly Monroe used novelty print fabrics to piece her quilt top, which is accented with whimsical talking flowers.

PROJECT RATING: INTERMEDIATE
Size: 44½" × 44½"
Blocks: 16 (8⅝") blocks

MATERIALS

14 fat quarters★ novelty prints
¼ yard red print
1 yard gold solid
1 fat quarter★ green solid
Scraps of red, blue, purple, pink solid
⅜ yard black print for binding
Paper-backed fusible web
Fons & Porter Half & Quarter
  Ruler (optional)
White and Black Opaque paint
  markers
3 yards backing fabric
Twin-size quilt batting
★fat quarter = 18" × 20"

Cutting

If not using the Fons & Porter Half & Quarter Ruler, pattern for C triangle is on page 124. Measurements include ¼" seam allowances. Border strips are exact length needed. You may want to

make them longer to allow for piecing variations. Patterns for flowers and faces are on pages 124–125. Follow manufacturer's instructions for using fusible web.

From each novelty print fat quarter, cut:

• 3 (5"-wide) strips. From strips, cut wedges as shown in *Wedge Cutting Diagram.* Vary the wedges, cutting them no smaller than 1" at the narrow end and no larger than 1¾" at the wide end.

• 1 (1½"-wide) strip for strip sets.

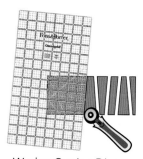

Wedge Cutting Diagram

From red print, cut:

• 4 (1½"-wide) strips. From strips, cut 2 (1½" × 37") top and bottom inner borders and 2 (1½" × 35") side inner borders.

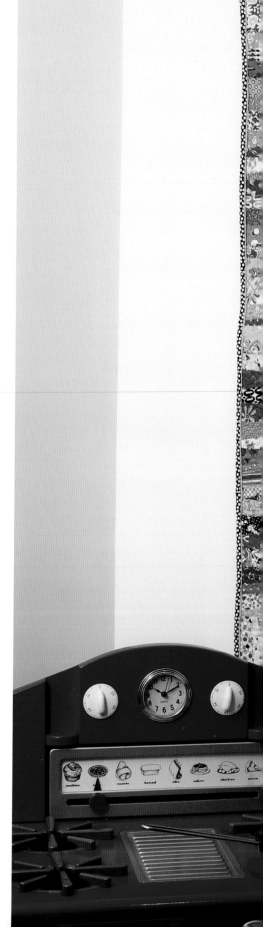

- -

From gold solid, cut:

- 3 (6⅝"-wide) strips. From strips, cut 16 (6⅝") squares. Cut squares in half diagonally to make 32 half-square B triangles.
- 9 (1"-wide) strips. From strips, cut 4 (1" × 37") strips for inner piping. Piece remaining strips to make 4 (1" × 45") strips for outer piping.

From green solid, cut:

- Stems, Arms, and Legs for all flowers.
- 1 Head for flower #4.

From assorted scraps, cut:

- Heads for flowers #1, #2, #3, and #5.

From black print, cut:

- 5 (2¼"-wide) strips for binding.

Block Assembly

1. Referring to *Unit A Assembly Diagrams*, join 9–10 wedges, alternating the narrow and wide ends of the wedges. Trim to 4½" × 8½" to complete 1 Unit A *(Unit A Diagram)*. Make 16 Unit A.

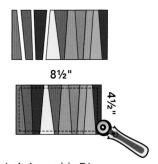

8½"

4½"

Unit A Assembly Diagrams

Unit A Diagram

2. Referring to *Strip Set Diagrams,* join 2 assorted 1½"-wide strips. Make 7 strip sets. From strip sets, cut 32 C triangles using the Fons & Porter Half & Quarter Ruler. Place ruler on strip set with strip width line marked 2½ aligned with bottom edge of strip set. Cut on both sides of ruler. Turn ruler and place on strip set with line marked 2½ on top edge of strip. Cut along right edge of ruler. Repeat to cut remaining triangles. If not using the Fons & Porter Half & Quarter Ruler, use template C on page 124.

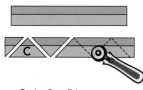

Strip Set Diagrams

3. Lay out 2 gold B triangles, 1 Unit A, and 2 C triangles as shown in *Block Assembly Diagram.* Join to complete 1 block *(Block Diagram)*. Make 16 blocks.

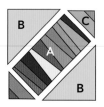

Block Assembly Diagram

Block Diagram

Pieced Border Assembly

1. Referring to *Unit A Assembly Diagrams,* join 40–45 wedges, alternating the narrow and wide ends of the wedges. Trim to 4½" × 37" to make 1 pieced side outer border. Make 2 pieced side outer borders.

2. In the same manner, join 50–55 wedges. Trim to 4½" × 45" to make 1 pieced top outer border. Repeat to make bottom outer border.

Quilt Assembly

1. Lay out blocks as shown in *Quilt Top Assembly Diagram.* Join into rows, join rows to complete quilt center.

2. Referring to photo on page 121, position stems, petals, faces, arms, and legs on quilt center. Fuse in place.

3. Machine appliqué pieces on quilt using matching thread and a small zigzag stitch.

4. Referring to photo on page 121 and patterns for faces on pages 124–125, draw face details using paint markers.

5. Add red print side inner borders to quilt center. Add red print top and bottom inner borders to quilt.

6. Fold 1 inner piping strip in half lengthwise with wrong sides facing. Matching raw edges, baste piping strip to 1 side of quilt center. Repeat for remaining side. Repeat for top and bottom.

7. Add pieced side outer borders to quilt, stitching through all layers. Add pieced top and bottom borders to quilt.

8. Fold 1 outer piping strip in half lengthwise with wrong sides facing. Matching raw edges, baste piping strip to 1 side of quilt. Repeat for remining side. Repeat for top and bottom.

Finishing

1. Divide backing into 2 (1½-yard) lengths. Cut 1 piece in half lengthwise to make 2 narrow panels. Join 1 narrow panel to wider panel. Remaining panel is extra and can be used to make a hanging sleeve.

2. Layer backing, batting, and quilt top; baste. Quilt as desired. Quilt shown was quilted with freehand curves in the gold areas, and with meandering in the pieced borders *(Quilting Diagram)*.

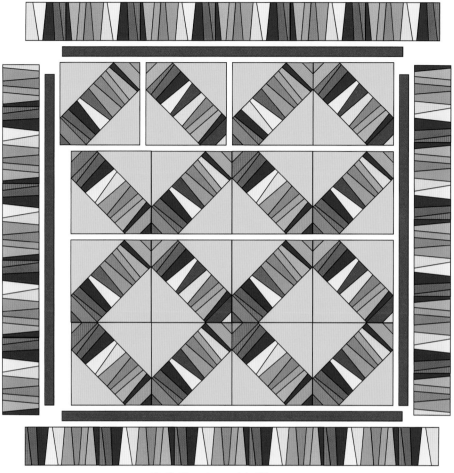

Quilt Top Assembly Diagram

DESIGNER

Kelly Monroe from Arlington, Texas remembers the first quilt she ever made. "It wasn't too pretty, but I was hooked," she said. "I've learned to 'clean up my act' and now I love to work in the brightest and boldest colors." Kelly's inspiration came from her love of the antique look of 1930s reproduction fabrics. She added yellow to make the quilt nice and bright for baby. ✳

3. Join 2¼"-wide black print strips into 1 continuous piece for straight-grain French-fold binding. Add binding to quilt.

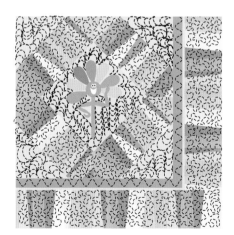

Quilting Diagram

TRIED & TRUE

Not ready for appliqué? The Feather & Furry Friends collection by Vintage Workshop for Red Rooster Fabrics, makes a great choice for an easier version of this quilt.

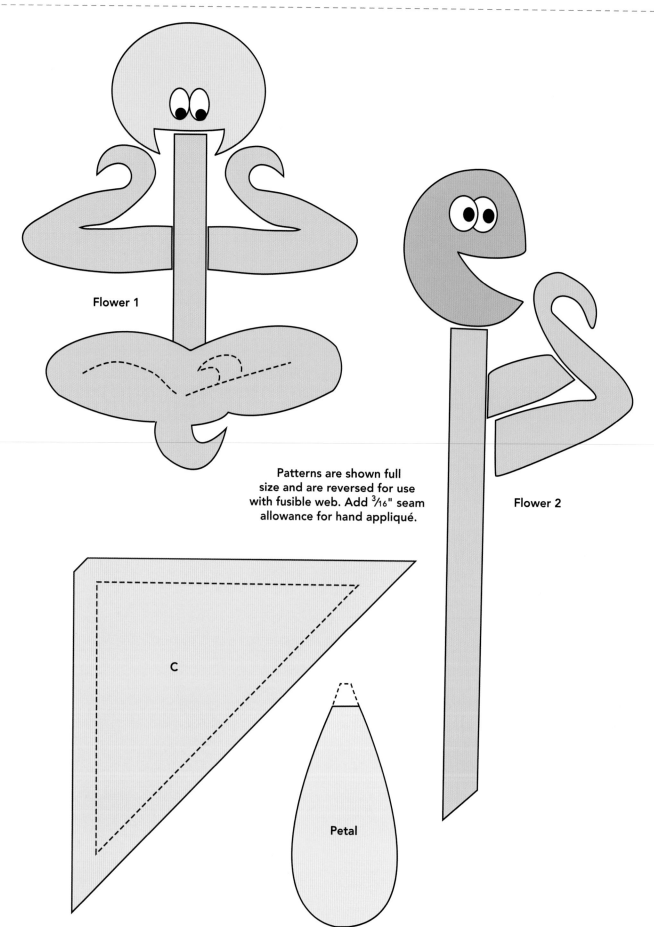

Flower 1

Flower 2

Patterns are shown full
size and are reversed for use
with fusible web. Add $^3/_{16}$" seam
allowance for hand appliqué.

C

Petal

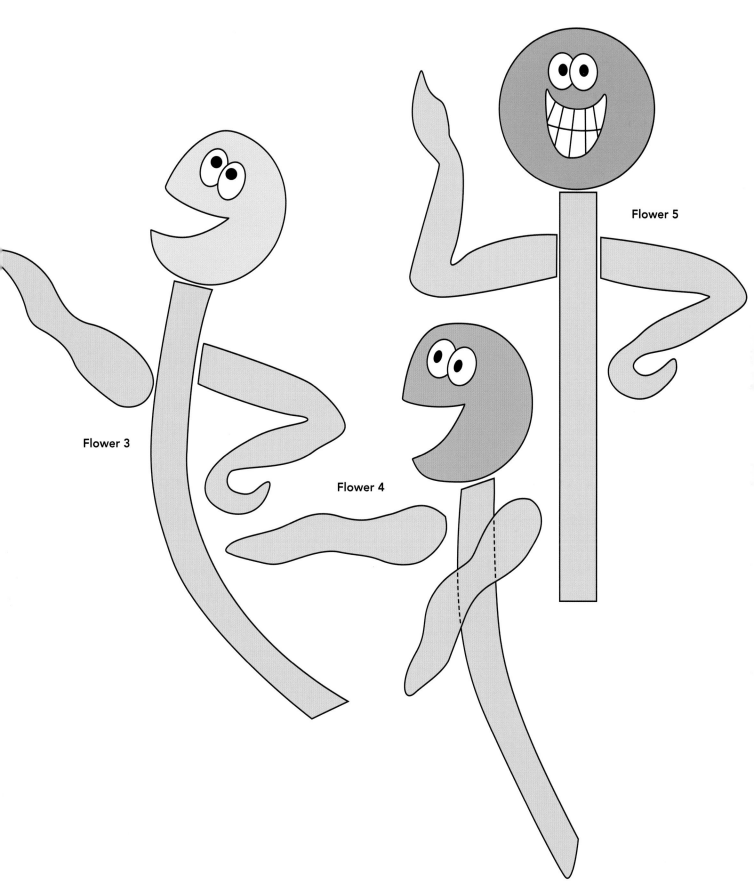

Flower 5

Flower 3

Flower 4

Training Wheels

This old favorite is made with fresh fabrics. The bold contemporary prints bring motion to these little training wheels.

PROJECT RATING: CHALLENGING
Size: 48" × 53½"

MATERIALS

6 fat quarters* assorted pink and
   green prints for blocks
1½ yards light yellow print for
   blocks
¾ yard dark yellow print #1 for
   block centers and binding
⅜ yard dark yellow print #2 for
   inner border
¾ yard green print for outer border
Paper-backed fusible web
3½ yards backing fabric
Fons &Porter's Wagon Wheel
   Template Set or template material
Twin-size quilt batting
*fat quarter = 18" × 20"

NOTE: Fabrics in the quilt shown are from the Mingle collection by Monaluna for Kaufman Fabrics.

Cutting

If you are not using the Wagon Wheel Template Set, make templates from the patterns on page 129. Punch hole in B template at point indicated by dot on pattern piece. Measurements include ¼" seam allowances. Follow manufacturer's instructions for using fusible web.

From each fat quarter, cut:
• 28 A.

From light yellow print, cut:
• 157 B.

From dark yellow print #1, cut:
• 33 Centers.
• 6 (2¼"-wide) strips for binding.

From dark yellow print #2, cut:
• 5 (2"-wide) strips for inner border.

From green print, cut:
• 5 (4½"-wide) strips for outer border.

Wheel Assembly

1. Choose 6 assorted A pieces and 6 light yellow print B pieces. Mark dot on each B piece. Join 3 A pieces and 3 B pieces as shown in *Wheel Diagrams* to make a hexagon half. Make 2 halves; join to complete 1 hexagon.

2. Position 1 Center atop hexagon, covering raw edges of A and B pieces. Fuse in place.

> **Sew Smart**™
> Work on an appliqué pressing sheet when fusing so you don't get fusible residue on your ironing surface. —Marianne

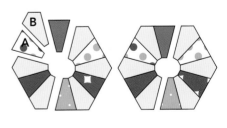

Wheel Diagrams

3. Using matching thread and a decorative machine stitch, appliqué Center on hexagon to complete 1 Wheel. Make 18 Wheels.

4. In the same manner, make 11 X Half Wheels and 4 Y Half Wheels *(Half Wheel Diagrams)*.

X Half Wheel   **Y Half Wheel**

Half Wheel Diagrams

Quilt Assembly

1. Lay out Wheels and Half Wheels as shown in *Quilt Top Assembly Diagram*. Join into vertical rows, stitching from dot to dot and backstitching at dots; leaving seam allowance free beyond dots. In the same manner, join rows to complete quilt center.

2. Trim edges of quilt top to straighten as shown in *Quilt Top Assembly Diagram*.

3. Measure length of quilt center. Make 2 side inner borders this measurement using dark yellow #2 print strips. Add borders to quilt.

4. Measure width of quilt center (including side borders). Make 2 top and bottom inner borders this measurement using dark yellow #2 print strips. Add borders to quilt.

5. Repeat steps #3 and #4 for outer borders, using green print strips.

Finishing

1. Divide backing into 2 (1¾-yard) lengths. Cut 1 piece in half lengthwise to make 2 narrow panels. Join 1 narrow panel to wider panel. Remaining panel is extra and can be used to make a hanging sleeve.

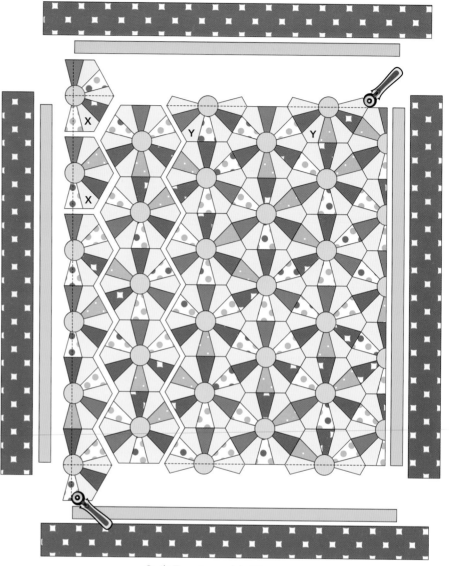

Quilt Top Assembly Diagram

2. Layer backing, batting, and quilt top; baste. Quilt as desired. Quilt shown was quilted in the ditch and with straight lines in the outer border. *(Quilting Diagram)*.

3. Join 2¼"-wide dark yellow print #1 strips into 1 continuous piece for straight-grain French-fold binding. Add binding to quilt.

Quilting Diagram

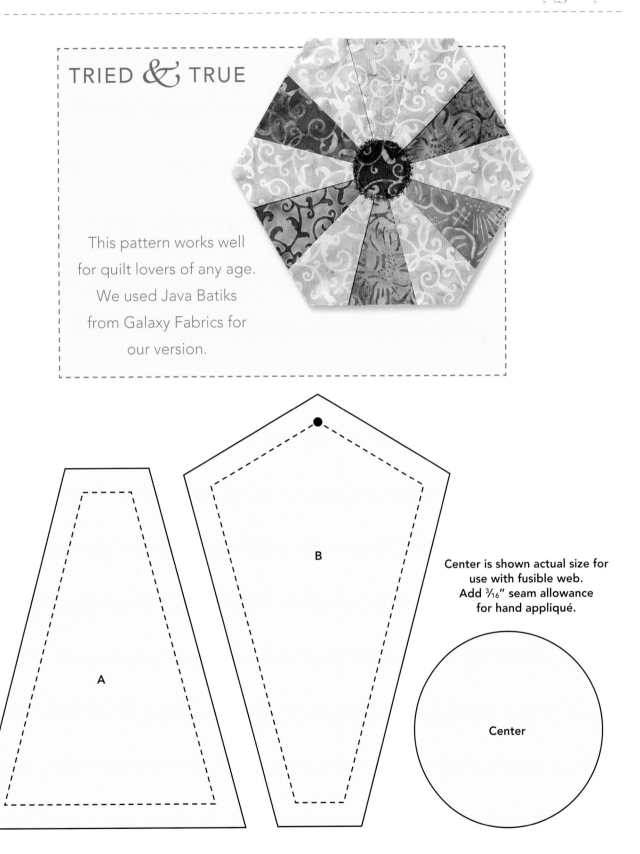

TRIED & TRUE

This pattern works well for quilt lovers of any age. We used Java Batiks from Galaxy Fabrics for our version.

A

B

Center is shown actual size for use with fusible web. Add $3/16$" seam allowance for hand appliqué.

Center

Meow

Machine appliqué cute kitties in 1930s reproduction prints.

Size: 38" × 38"

Blocks: 9 (9") Cat blocks

MATERIALS

1 yard yellow print for blocks

5 fat eighths★ assorted prints in blue, green, lavender, yellow, and peach

½ yard blue print for sashing and middle border

1 yard red print for block, inner and outer borders, and binding

10" square pink print for noses and ears

6" square each brown and white solid for eyes

Paper-backed fusible web

Black Embroidery Floss

1¼ yards backing fabric

Crib-size quilt batting

★fat eighth = 9" × 20"

NOTE: Fabrics in the quilt shown are from the Storybook VII collection by Windham Fabrics.

Cutting

Measurements include ¼" seam allowances. Border strips are exact length needed. You may want to make them longer to allow for piecing variations. Patterns for appliqué are on page 133. Follow manufacturer's instructions for using fusible web.

From yellow print, cut:

- 3 (9½"-wide) strips. From strips, cut 9 (9½") block background squares.

From assorted print fat eighths, cut a total of:

- 8 Heads.
- 8 Front Bodies.
- 8 Back Bodies.
- 8 Tails.

From blue print, cut:

- 4 (2½"-wide) strips. From strips, cut 2 (2½" × 35½") top and bottom middle borders and 2 (2½" × 31½") side middle borders.
- 3 (1½"-wide) strips. From strips, cut 12 (1½" × 9½") sashing rectangles.

From red print, cut:

- 5 (2¼"-wide) strips for binding.
- 4 (2"-wide) strips. From strips, cut 2 (2" × 38½") top and bottom outer borders and 2 (2" × 35½") side outer borders.

- 4 (1½"-wide) strips. From strips, cut 2 (1½" × 31½") top and bottom inner borders, 2 (1½" × 29½") side inner borders, and 4 (1½") sashing squares.
- 1 Head.
- 1 Front Body.
- 1 Back Body.
- 1 Tail.

From pink print, cut:

- 9 Left Ears.
- 9 Right Ears.
- 9 Noses.

From brown solid, cut:

- 18 Eye Circles.

From white solid, cut:

- 18 Eyes.

Block Assembly

1. Referring to *Block Diagram*, arrange 1 Tail, 1 Back Body, 1 Front Body, 1 Head, 2 white Eyes, 2 brown Eye Circles, 1 Left Ear, 1 Right Ear, and 1 Nose on 1 yellow print square. Fuse in place.

Block Diagram

2. Machine appliqué pieces using blanket stitch and matching thread to complete 1 block. Make 9 blocks.

3. Embroider mouth using black embroidery floss and back stitch *(Back Stitch Diagram)*.

Back Stitch Diagram

Quilt Assembly

1. Lay out blocks, blue print sashing rectangles, and red print sashing squares as shown in *Quilt Top Assembly Diagram*. Join into rows; join rows to complete quilt center.

2. Add red print side inner borders to quilt center. Add red print top and bottom inner borders to quilt.

3. Repeat for blue print middle borders and red print outer borders.

Finishing

1. Layer backing, batting, and quilt top; baste. Quilt as desired. Quilt shown was quilted with meandering in the blocks and in the ditch around borders *(Quilting Diagram)*.

2. Join 2¼"-wide red print strips into 1 continuous piece for straight-grain French-fold binding. Add binding to quilt.

Quilt Top Assembly Diagram

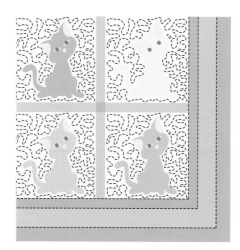

Quilting Diagram

TRIED & TRUE

We made our kitty with a mottled, fur-like print. He would look cute in plaids or polka dots, too!

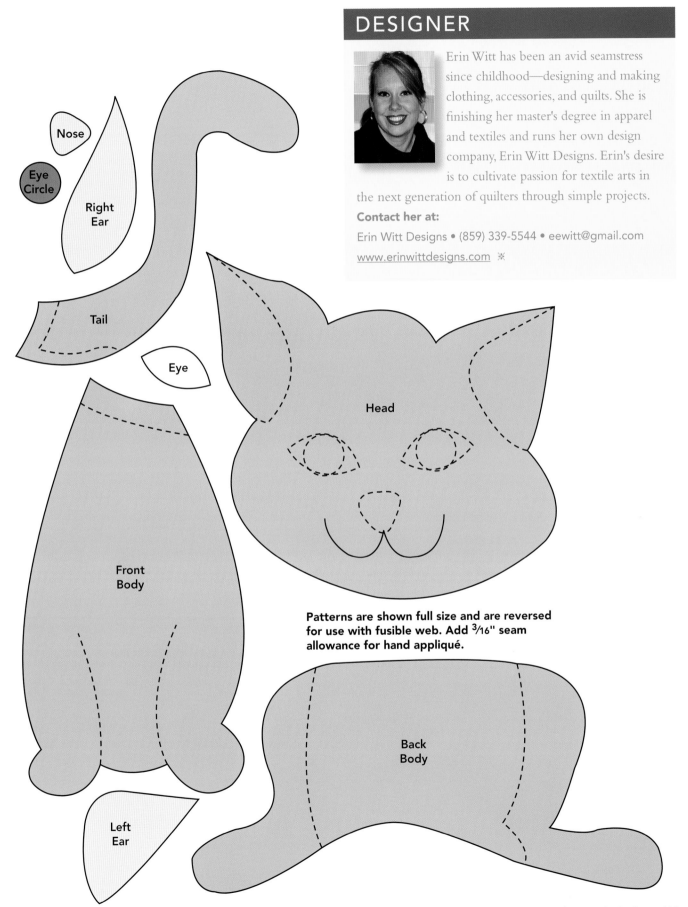

Nose

Eye
Circle

Right
Ear

Tail

Eye

Head

Front
Body

DESIGNER

Erin Witt has been an avid seamstress since childhood—designing and making clothing, accessories, and quilts. She is finishing her master's degree in apparel and textiles and runs her own design company, Erin Witt Designs. Erin's desire is to cultivate passion for textile arts in the next generation of quilters through simple projects.

Contact her at:

Erin Witt Designs • (859) 339-5544 • eewitt@gmail.com
www.erinwittdesigns.com ❋

Patterns are shown full size and are reversed for use with fusible web. Add 3/16" seam allowance for hand appliqué.

Back
Body

Left
Ear

Teddy and Friends

Appliqué endearing calico teddy bears onto a little quilt to wrap around baby.
Three-dimensional ears add a special touch.

PROJECT RATING: INTERMEDIATE
Size: 48" × 48"
Blocks: 9 (10") Teddy blocks

MATERIALS

9 fat quarters★ assorted prints for
  Teddy blocks
1 fat eighth★★ red print for hearts
1 fat eighth★★ brown print for
  noses
1 fat eighth★★ black solid for eyes
1¾ yards cream solid for blocks and
  pieced border
1¼ yards pink print for sashing,
  borders, and binding
⅝ yard green print for pieced
  border
Paper-backed fusible web
3 yards backing fabric
Twin-size quilt batting
★fat quarter = 18" × 20"
★★fat eighth = 9" × 20"

NOTE: Fabrics in the quilt shown are
from the Granny's Treasures collection by
Nancy Mahoney for P&B Textiles.

Cutting

Measurements include ¼" seam
allowances. Border strips are exact
length needed. You may want to make
them longer to allow for piecing
variations. Appliqué patterns are on page
137. Follow manufacturer's instructions
for using fusible web.

From each fat quarter, cut:
• 1 Head.
• 1 Body.
• 4 Ears.
• 2 Arms.
• 1 Leg.
• 1 Leg reversed.
• 2 Feet.

From red print fat eighth, cut:
• 9 Hearts.

From brown print fat eighth, cut:
• 9 Snouts.

From black solid fat eighth, cut:
• 9 Noses.
• 18 Eyes.

From cream solid, cut:
• 3 (10½"-wide) strips. From strips, cut
  9 (10½") squares.
• 12 (2"-wide) strips for strip sets.

From pink print, cut:
• 5 (2½"-wide) strips. Piece strips to
  make 2 (2½" × 48½") top and bottom
  outer borders and 2 (2½" × 44½")
  side outer borders.
• 6 (2¼"-wide) strips for binding.
• 4 (2"-wide) strips. From strips, cut 2
  (2" × 35½") top and bottom inner
  borders and 2 (2" × 32½") side inner
  borders.
• 4 (1½"-wide) strips. From strips, cut 2
  (1½" × 32½") E sashing strips and 6
  (1½" × 10½") D sashing strips.

From green print, cut:
• 9 (2"-wide) strips for strip sets.

Block Assembly

1. Place 2 Ears right sides facing. Stitch with ¼" seam, leaving base open for turning. Turn right side out and press to complete 1 ear. Make 9 sets of 2 matching ears.

2. Position 1 set of matching Teddy Bear parts on 1 cream print square, tucking Ears under Head.

3. Machine appliqué using matching thread to complete 1 Teddy block *(Block Diagram)*. Make 9 blocks.

Block Diagram

Pieced Border Assembly

1. Join 2 green print strips and 1 cream solid strip as shown in *Strip Set #1 Diagram*. Make 2 Strip Set #1. From strip sets, cut 32 (2"-wide) A segments.

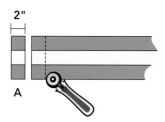

Strip Set #1 Diagram

2. Join 2 cream solid strips and 1 green print strip as shown in *Strip Set #2 Diagrams*. Make 5 Strip Set #2. From strip sets, cut 16 (5⅞"-wide) B segments and 16 (2"-wide) C segments.

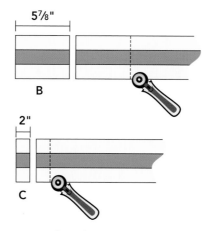

Strip Set #2 Diagrams

3. Join 2 A segments and 1 C segment as shown in *Nine Patch Unit Diagrams*. Make 16 Nine Patch Units.

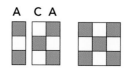

Nine Patch Unit Diagrams

4. Lay out 4 B segments and 3 Nine Patch Units as shown in *Quilt Top Assembly Diagram*. Join to make 1 Pieced Border. Make 4 Pieced Borders.

Quilt Assembly

1. Lay out blocks and pink print D and E sashing strips as shown in *Quilt Top Assembly Diagram*. Join into rows; join rows to complete quilt center.

2. Add pink print side inner borders to quilt center. Add pink print top and bottom inner borders to quilt.

3. Add pieced borders to sides of quilt. Join 1 Nine Patch Unit to each end of remaining pieced borders. Add borders to top and bottom of quilt.

4. Add pink print side outer borders to quilt center. Add pink print top and bottom outer borders to quilt.

Quilt Top Assembly Diagram

Finishing

1. Divide backing into 2 (1½-yard) lengths. Cut 1 piece in half lengthwise to make 2 narrow panels. Join 1 narrow panel to wider panel. Remaining panel is extra and can be used to make a hanging sleeve.

2. Layer backing, batting, and quilt top; baste. Quilt as desired. Quilt shown was quilted in the ditch and outline quilted around appliqué. Borders are quilted with parallel lines *(Quilting Diagram)*.

3. Join 2¼"-wide pink print strips into 1 continuous piece for straight-grain French-fold binding. Add binding to quilt.

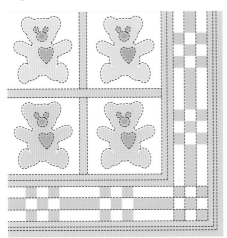

Quilting Diagram

DESIGNER

A prolific quiltmaker and author of eleven books, Nancy Mahoney is also a teacher and fabric designer. She enjoys making traditional quilts using new techniques that make quiltmaking easy and fun.

Contact her at:
www.nancymahoney.com ❋

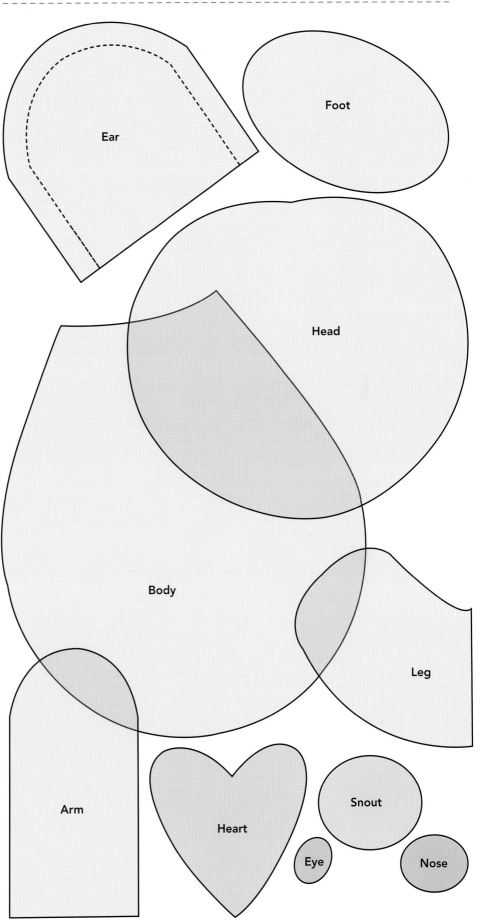

Baby Barnyard

Farm animals peek out from 3-dimensional barn doors to surprise youngsters.

PROJECT RATING: INTERMEDIATE

Size: 58" × 58"

Blocks: 9 (12") Patch blocks

MATERIALS

3 yards pasture print

1 fat eighth★ each cow, horse, pig, sheep, chicken, and egg prints

1 yard blue print for sky

1½ yards red print for barns

1 fat quarter★★ green print for grass

1⅜ yards black print #1 for roofs, shutters, doors, and binding

⅝ yard black print #2 for sashing and inner border

Paper-backed fusible web

18 (½"-diameter) black buttons

Black perle cotton

3½ yards backing fabric

Twin-size quilt batting

★fat eighth = 9" × 20"

★★fat quarter = 18" × 20"

NOTE: Fabrics in the quilt shown are from the Barnyard and Barnyard II collections by Blank Quilting.

Cutting

Measurements include ¼" seam allowances. Border strips are exact length needed. You may want to make them longer to allow for piecing variations. Pattern for Roof is on page 141. Follow manufacturer's instructions for using fusible web.

NOTE: Buttons on this quilt may present a choking hazard for children.

From pasture print, cut:

• 8 (8½"-wide) strips. Piece strips, matching design, to make 4 (8½" × 62") outer borders.

NOTE: Cut identical strips, centering same section of design in each.

From chicken print fat eighth, cut:

• 2 (2½"-wide) strips. From strips, cut 9 (2½" × 3½") C rectangles.

From egg print fat eighth, cut:

• 1 (2½"-wide) strip. From strip, cut 4 (2½") sashing squares.

From each remaining fat eighth, cut:

• 1 (4½"-wide) strip. From strips, cut a total of 9 (4½" × 5½") A rectangles.

From blue print, cut:

• 3 (5½"-wide) strips. From strips, cut 18 (5½") G squares.

• 9 (1½"-wide) strips. From strips, cut 9 (1½" × 12½") I rectangles and 18 (1½" × 10½") H rectangles.

From red print, cut:

• 2 (4½"-wide) strips. From strips, cut 18 (4½" × 3") B rectangles.

• 3 (4¼"-wide) strips. From strips, cut 36 (4¼" × 3") J rectangles.

• 3 (3½"-wide) strips. From strips, cut 9 (3½" × 10½") E rectangles.

• 2 (2½"-wide) strips. From strips, cut 18 (2½" × 4") D rectangles.

• 3 (1½"-wide) strips. From strips, cut 9 (1½" × 10½") F rectangles.

From green print fat quarter, cut:

• 9 (1½"-wide) **lengthwise** strips. From strips, cut 9 (1½" × 12½") I rectangles.

From black print #1, cut:

• 9 (2¼"-wide) strips. From 2 strips, cut 36 (2¼" × 2") K rectangles. Remaining strips are for binding.

• 11 (⅝"-wide) strips. From strips, cut 72 (⅝" × 5¼") L rectangles.

NOTE: Apply fusible web to fabric before cutting strips for L rectangles.

• 9 Roofs.

From black print #2, cut:

• 4 (2½"-wide) strips. From strips, cut 12 (2½" × 12½") sashing rectangles.

• 5 (1½"-wide) strips. Piece strips to make 2 (1½" × 40½") side inner borders and 2 (1½" × 42½") top and bottom inner borders.

Block Assembly

1. Position 2 black print #1 L strips on 1 red print J rectangle as shown in *Door Unit Diagram*. Fuse in place; machine appliqué using black thread. Make 36 Door Units. Trim ends of L rectangles even with edges of J rectangle.

Door Unit Diagram

2. Layer 2 door units right sides facing. Stitch 2 short sides and one long side as shown in *Door Diagram*. Turn right side out; press to complete 1 door. Make 18 doors.

Door Diagram

3. Layer 2 black print #1 K rectangles right sides facing. Stitch 2 short sides and one long side as shown in *Shutter Diagram*. Turn right side out; press to complete 1 shutter. Make 18 shutters.

Shutter Diagram

4. Center and baste 2 doors to 1 animal print A rectangle, aligning raw edges as shown in *Lower Barn Assembly Diagrams*. Stitch 1 red print B rectangle to each side of animal print A rectangle. Open to reveal doors; press.

Lower Barn Assembly Diagrams

5. In a similar manner, baste 2 shutters to chicken print C rectangle as shown in *Window Unit Assembly Diagrams*. Add 2 red print D rectangles to chicken print C rectangle. Open to reveal window; press. Add red print E rectangle to top, being careful not to catch shutters in seam *(Window Unit Diagram)*.

Window Unit Assembly Diagrams

Window Unit Diagram

6. Referring to *Diagonal Seams Diagrams*, place 1 blue print G square atop Window Unit, right sides facing. Stitch diagonally from corner to corner as shown. Trim ¼" beyond stitching. Press open to reveal triangle. Repeat for other end to complete Upper Barn Unit *(Upper Barn Unit Diagram)*.

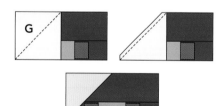

Diagonal Seams Diagrams

Upper Barn Unit Diagram

7. Join Lower Barn Unit, 1 red print F rectangle, and 1 Upper Barn Unit as shown in *Block Assembly Diagram*. Add 1 blue print H rectangle to each side, 1 blue print I rectangle to top, and 1 green print I rectangle to bottom of block.

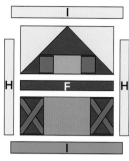

Block Assembly Diagram

8. Hand tack shutters open using black thread.

9. Fuse 1 black print roof to block. Machine appliqué roof to complete 1 Barn block *(Block Diagram)*. Make 9 Barn blocks.

Block Diagram

Quilt Assembly

1. Lay out blocks, sashing rectangles, and sashing squares as shown in *Quilt Top Assembly Diagram*. Join into rows; join rows to complete quilt center.

2. Add black print #2 side inner borders to quilt center. Add top and bottom inner borders to quilt.

3. Add outer borders to quilt, mitering corners. See *Sew Easy: Mitered Borders* on page 163 for instructions.

Finishing

1. Divide backing into 2 (1¾-yard) lengths. Cut 1 piece in half lengthwise to make 2 narrow panels. Join 1 narrow panel to each side of wider panel; press seam allowances toward narrow panels.

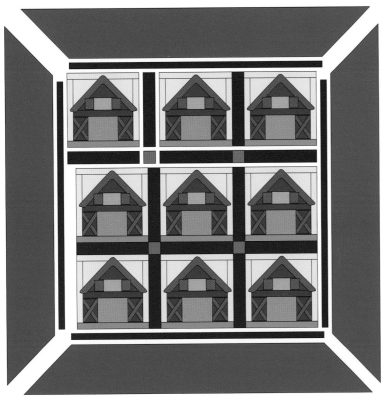

Quilt Top Assembly Diagram

2. Layer backing, batting, and quilt top; baste. Quilt as desired. Quilt shown was quilted in the ditch and along lines in outer border *(Quilting Diagram)*.

3. Join 2¼"-wide black print #1 print strips into 1 continuous piece for straight-grain French-fold binding. Add binding to quilt.

4. Add 1 button to each door. Attach a loop of black perle cotton to each left door button. Slip loop over right door button to close door.

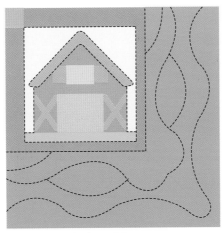

Quilting Diagram

DESIGNER

Heidi Pridemore, owner of The Whimsical Workshop in Chandler, Arizona, is known for her fun quilts. She has designed hundreds of quilt patterns and written five books, and also designs fabric.

Contact her at:

info@TheWhimsicalWorkshop.com

www.TheWhimsicalWorkshop.com ❋

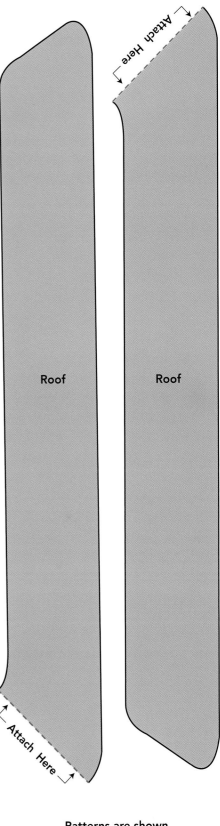

Attach Here

Roof   Roof

Attach Here

Patterns are shown full size for use with fusible web. Add ³⁄₁₆" seam allowance for hand appliqué.

QUILT BY **Jackie Robinson**.
MACHINE QUILTED BY **Carole Moseley**.

Rootin' Tootin' Cowboy

Jackie Robinson created this classic old-west cowboy quilt. Boots are cleverly pieced inside the center stars, and a feather print border provides the perfect frame.

PROJECT RATING: EASY
Size: 65" × 97"
Blocks: 8 (8") blocks

MATERIALS

3 yards tan stripe for border
2½ yards tan print
½ yard red print
1⅛ yards dark red print
½ yard blue print
⅝ yard dark blue print
⅛ yard gold print
6 yards backing fabric
Queen-size quilt batting

NOTE: Fabrics in the quilt shown are from the Cowboys & Indians collection by Maywood Studio.

Cutting

Measurements include ¼" seam allowances.

From tan stripe, cut:
- 4 (8¾"-wide) **lengthwise** strips, centering stripe in each. From strips, cut 2 (8¾" × 103") side borders and 2 (8¾" × 72") top and bottom borders.

From tan print, cut:
- 2 (8⅞"-wide) strips. From strips, cut 8 (8⅞") squares. Cut squares in half diagonally to make 16 half-square M triangles.
- 3 (8½"-wide) strips. From strips, cut 2 (8½" × 16½") L rectangles and 8 (8½") K squares.
- 6 (4½"-wide) strips. From strips, cut 48 (4½") J squares.
- 6 (2½"-wide) strips for strip sets.

From red print, cut:
- 1 (5½"-wide) strip. From strip, cut 8 (5½" × 4") B rectangles.
- 3 (2½"-wide) strips for strip sets.

From dark red print, cut:
- 3 (2½"-wide) strips for strip sets.
- 9 (2¼"-wide) strips for binding.

- 3 (2"-wide) strips. From strips, cut 8 (2" × 5½") D rectangles and 8 (2" × 6½") I rectangles.

From blue print, cut:
- 1 (5½"-wide) strip. From strip, cut 8 (5½" × 5") C rectangles.
- 2 (2"-wide) strips. From strips, cut 16 (2") H squares, 8 (2" × 5") E rectangles, and 8 (2" × 1") F rectangles.
- 1 (1½"-wide) strip. From strip, cut 16 (1½") A squares.

From dark blue print, cut:
- 2 (8⅞"-wide) strips. From strips, cut 8 (8⅞") squares. Cut squares in half diagonally to make 16 half-square M triangles.

From gold print, cut:
- 1 (2"-wide) strip. From strip, cut 8 (2" × 2½") G rectangles.

Block Assembly

1. Referring to *Shank Unit Diagrams*, place 1 blue print A square atop 1 red print B rectangle, right sides facing. Stitch diagonally from corner to corner as shown. Trim ¼" beyond stitching.

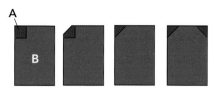

Shank Unit Diagrams

Press open to reveal triangle. Repeat for adjacent top corner to complete 1 Shank Unit. Make 8 Shank Units.

2. Referring to *Toe Unit Diagrams,* use the diagonal seams method to stitch 1 blue print H square to each end of 1 dark red I rectangle to complete 1 Toe Unit. Make 8 Toe Units.

Toe Unit Diagrams

3. Referring to *Boot Unit Diagrams*, use the diagonal seams method to join 1 dark red print D rectangle and 1 blue print E rectangle as shown to make 1 Boot Unit. Make 8 Boot Units.

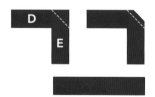

Boot Unit Diagrams

4. Referring to *Heel Unit Diagrams,* place 1 blue print F rectangle atop 1 gold print G rectangle with right sides facing.

NOTE: Top corner of F rectangle is aligned with top corner of G rectangle, and opposite corner of F rectangle is aligned with bottom edge of G rectangle 1" from corner.

Heel Unit Diagrams

5. Draw a line diagonally from corner to corner as shown. Stitch on drawn line. Trim ¼" beyond stitching. Press open to reveal triangle to complete 1 Heel Unit. Make 8 Heel Units.

6. Lay out 1 Shank Unit, 1 blue print C rectangle, 1 Boot Unit, 1 Heel Unit, and 1 Toe Unit as shown in *Block Assembly Diagram.* Join units into rows; join rows to complete 1 block *(Block Diagram).* Make 8 blocks.

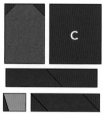 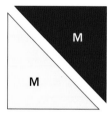 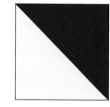

Block Assembly   Block Diagram
Diagram

Quilt Assembly

1. Join 1 dark blue print M triangle and 1 tan print M triangle as shown in *Triangle-Square Diagrams.* Make 16 triangle-squares.

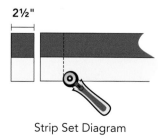

Triangle-Squares Diagram

2. Join 1 tan print strip and 1 red print strip as shown in *Strip Set Diagram.* Make 3 red strip sets. From strip sets, cut 48 (2½"-wide) red segments.

Strip Set Diagram

3. In the same manner, join 1 tan print strip and 1 dark red print strip. Make 3 dark red strip sets. From strip sets, cut 48 (2½"-wide) dark red segments.

4. Lay out 2 red segments, 2 dark red segments, and 2 tan print J squares as shown in *Four Patch Unit Diagrams.* Join into rows; join rows to complete 1 Four Patch Unit. Make 24 Four Patch Units.

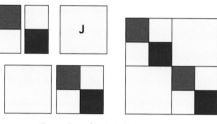

Four Patch Unit Diagrams

5. Lay out Four Patch Units, tan print K squares and L rectangles, triangle-squares, and blocks as shown in *Quilt Top Assembly Diagram.* Join into rows; join rows to complete quilt center.

6. Add borders to quilt center, mitering corners. See *Sew Easy: Mitered Borders* on page 163 for instructions.

Finishing

1. Divide backing into 2 (3-yard) lengths. Cut 1 piece in half lengthwise to make 2 narrow panels. Join 1 narrow panel to each side of wider panel; press seam allowances toward narrow panels.

2. Layer backing, batting, and quilt top; baste. Quilt as desired. Quilt shown was outline quilted around the feathers in the border stripe, has diagonal lines through the Four Patch Units, and has boot, hat, horse, and star designs in the background *(Quilting Diagram).*

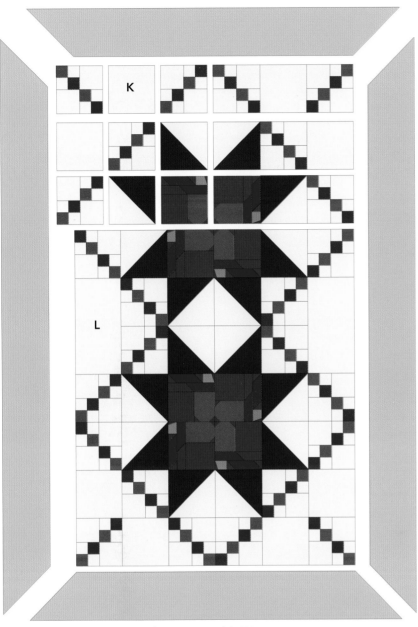

Quilt Top Assembly Diagram

3. Join 2¼"-wide dark red print strips into 1 continuous piece for straight-grain French-fold binding. Add binding to quilt.

Quilt Top Assembly Diagram

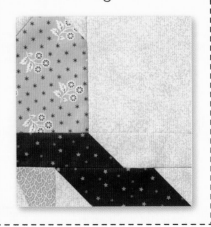
DESIGNER

Jackie Robinson is best known for her detailed, yet easy to make, pieced quilt designs. An international teacher and lecturer, Jackie has authored twelve quilting books and over 200 patterns. She also designs fabric. Her quilts have been exhibited in numerous shows, and have appeared in many magazines. Jackie was awarded the 2006 Jewel Pierce Patterson scholarship for quilt teachers. She now lives in scenic northwestern Montana with her husband, Jery Wyatt.

Contact her at: Animas Quilts • 830 Douglas Hill Road • Eureka, MT 59917 • www.animasquilts.com ❋

Trip Around the Rodeo

Do you know a horse-loving cowgirl? She is sure to love this quilt and matching pillowcases.

PROJECT RATING: EASY
Size: 80" × 96"
Blocks: 63 (8") blocks

MATERIALS

1½ yards cowgirl print for blocks

3½ yards beige print for blocks and borders

1⅛ yards light pink print for blocks and border

1 yard dark pink print for blocks and border

1⅛ yards gold print for blocks and border

⅝ yard light blue print for blocks

1⅛ yards dark blue print for blocks and border

⅝ yard green print for blocks

¾ yard tan print for binding

Fons & Porter Flying Geese Ruler (optional)

Fons & Porter Triangle Trimmers (optional)

7½ yards backing fabric

6⅛" square template plastic

Full-size quilt batting

NOTE: Fabrics in the quilt shown are from the You Go Girl collection by Dawn of Sun Valley Quilts for Northcott.

Cutting

Measurements include ¼" seam allowances. Border strips are exact length needed. You may want to make them longer to allow for piecing variations. Instructions are written for using the Fons & Porter Flying Geese Ruler. See *Sew Easy: Making Flying Geese Units* on page 151. If not using this ruler, follow cutting **NOTES**.

From cowgirl print, cut:

• 15 (6⅛") A squares on point, centering cowgirl in each. Place template plastic square atop fabric; draw around template. Cut on drawn line.

From beige print, cut:

• 8 (8½"-wide) strips. Piece strips to make 4 (8½" × 72½") inner borders.

• 3 (6⅛"-wide) strips. From strips, cut 16 (6⅛") A squares.

• 7 (4½"-wide) strips. From strips, cut 40 quarter-square C triangles and 4 half-square B triangles.

NOTE: If not using the Fons & Porter Flying Geese Ruler, cut 3 (9¼"-wide) strips. From strips, cut 10 (9¼") squares. Cut squares in half diagonally in both directions to make 40 quarter-square C triangles. Also cut 1 (4⅞"-wide) strip. From strip, cut 2 (4⅞") squares. Cut squares in half diagonally to make 4 half-square B triangles.

From light pink print, cut:

• 7 (4½"-wide) strips. From strips, cut 85 half-square B triangles.

NOTE: If not using the Fons & Porter Flying Geese Ruler, cut 6 (4⅞"-wide) strips. From strips, cut 43 (4⅞") squares. Cut squares in half diagonally to make 86 half-square B triangles (1 is extra).

From dark pink print, cut:

• 6 (4½"-wide) strips. From strips, cut 81 half-square B triangles.

NOTE: If not using the Fons & Porter Flying Geese Ruler, cut 6 (4⅞"-wide) strips. From strips, cut 41 (4⅞") squares. Cut squares in half diagonally to make 82 half-square B triangles (1 is extra).

From gold print, cut:

• 7 (4½"-wide) strips. From strips, cut 85 half-square B triangles.

NOTE: If not using the Fons & Porter Flying Geese Ruler, cut 6 (4⅞"-wide) strips. From strips, cut 43 (4⅞") squares. Cut squares in half diagonally to make 86 half-square B triangles (1 is extra).

From light blue print, cut:

• 3 (6⅛"-wide) strips. From strips, cut 16 (6⅛") A squares.

From dark blue print, cut:

• 7 (4½"-wide) strips. From strips, cut 85 half-square B triangles.

NOTE: If not using the Fons & Porter Flying Geese Ruler, cut 6 (4⅞"-wide) strips. From strips, cut 43 (4⅞") squares. Cut squares in half diagonally to make 86 half-square B triangles (1 is extra).

From green print, cut:

• 3 (6⅛"-wide) strips. From strips, cut 16 (6⅛") A squares.

From tan print, cut:

• 10 (2¼"-wide) strips for binding.

Block Assembly

1. Lay out 4 light pink B triangles and 1 beige print A square as shown in *Block Assembly Diagram.* Join to complete 1 block *(Block Diagrams)*. Make 16 light pink blocks.

> ### Sew Smart™
> Use the blue Fons & Porter Triangle Trimmer to trim B triangles. —Liz

Block Assembly Diagram

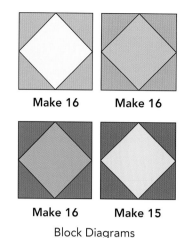

Make 16   Make 16

Make 16   Make 15

Block Diagrams

2. In the same manner, make 16 gold blocks using gold print B triangles and light blue print A squares, 16 blue blocks using dark blue print B triangles and green print A squares, and 15 dark pink blocks using dark pink B triangles and cowgirl print A squares.

Pieced Border Assembly

1. Join 1 gold print B triangle, 1 dark blue print B triangle, and 1 beige print C triangle as shown in *Flying Geese Unit Diagrams.* In the same manner, make Flying Geese Units in quantities as shown.

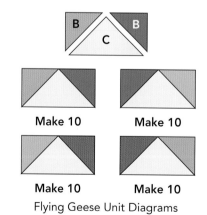

Make 10   Make 10

Make 10   Make 10

Flying Geese Unit Diagrams

2. Join 1 gold print B triangle and 1 beige print B triangle as shown in *Triangle-Square Diagrams.* In the same manner, make triangle-squares in quantities as shown.

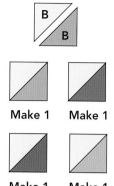

Make 1   Make 1

Make 1   Make 1

Triangle Square Diagrams

3. Lay out 10 Flying Geese Units and 2 triangle-squares as shown in *Quilt Top Assembly Diagram.* Join to make 1 pieced side border. Make 2 pieced side borders.

4. In the same manner, make pieced top border using 10 Flying Geese Units. Repeat for pieced bottom border.

Quilt Assembly

1. Lay out blocks as shown in *Quilt Top Assembly Diagram.* Join into rows; join rows to complete quilt center.

2. Add beige print side inner borders to quilt center. Add beige print top and bottom inner borders to quilt.

3. Repeat for pieced outer borders.

Finishing

1. Divide backing into 3 (2½-yard) lengths. Join panels lengthwise. Seams will run horizontally.

2. Layer backing, batting, and quilt top; baste. Quilt as desired. Quilt shown was quilted in the ditch and with orange peel and feather designs in the blocks *(Quilting Diagram)*.

3. Join 2¼"-wide tan print strips into 1 continuous piece for straight-grain French-fold binding. Add binding to quilt.

Quilt Top Assembly Diagram

Quilting Diagram

WEB EXTRA
Go to www.FonsandPorter.com/
triparoundtherodeosizes to
download *Quilt Top Assembly
Diagrams* for these size options.

**Directions for coordinating
pillowcases are on page 95.**

SIZE OPTIONS

	Crib (48" × 48")	Twin (64" × 96")
Blocks	9	45
Setting	3 × 3	5 × 9

MATERIALS

	Crib (48" × 48")	Twin (64" × 96")
Cowgirl Print	1 fat quarter★	1 yard
Beige Print	1¾ yards	3¼ yards
Light Pink Print	1 fat quarter★	¾ yard
Dark Pink Print	1 fat quarter★	¾ yard
Gold Print	⅜ yard	¾ yard
Light Blue Print	1 fat quarter★	½ yard
Dark Blue Print	⅜ yard	¾ yard
Green Print	1 fat quarter★	½ yard
Tan Print	½ yard	¾ yard
Backing Fabric	3 yards	6 yards
Batting	Twin-size	Queen-size

★fat quarter = 18" × 20"

DESIGNER

Patti Carey loves to design quilts using new collections, and hopes to inspire other quilters with her creations.

Contact her at: patti.carey@northcott.net ✳

Making Flying Geese Units

The Fons & Porter Flying Geese Ruler takes the guesswork out of cutting the triangles for Flying Geese Units. Both the large quarter-square triangle and the smaller half-square triangles are cut from the same width strips.

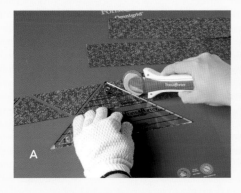

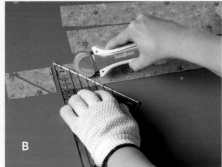

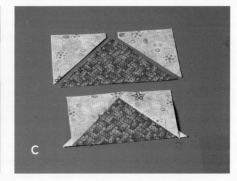

1. To cut the large quarter-square triangle, select black line on ruler that corresponds to the desired finished size Flying Geese Unit. (For the Flying Geese in *Trip Around the Rodeo* on page 146, the finished size is 4" × 8".)

2. Follow across black line to right edge of ruler and cut a fabric strip the width indicated. For example, to cut the large triangle for the 4" × 8" finished-size Flying Geese Unit, cut a 4½"-wide fabric strip.

3. Cut quarter-square triangles as shown in *Photo A*, first placing the black cutting guideline along bottom cut edge of strip and then along top edge of strip.

4. To cut the corresponding smaller half-square triangles, select the yellow line that corresponds to the desired finished size Flying Geese Unit.

5. Follow across yellow line to left edge of ruler and cut a fabric strip the width indicated. For example, to cut the small triangles for a 4" × 8" finished-size Flying Geese Unit, cut a 4½"-wide fabric strip.

6. Cut triangles as shown, first placing the yellow cutting guideline along bottom edge of strip and then along top edge (*Photo B*). The yellow shaded area of the ruler will extend beyond the edge of the strip.

Sew **Smart**™

Your triangles will be pre-trimmed with the tiny fabric tips that you usually cut off after sewing already eliminated. We cut triangles with the fabric strip folded in half so that half of the triangles are trimmed on the right end and the other half are trimmed on the left end (*Photo C*). —Liz

7. Join half-square triangles to center quarter-square triangle to complete 1 Flying Geese Unit.

Blast Off

Blast off to outer space and discover exciting constellations, orbit around the phases of the moon, and travel through glowing night skies.

PROJECT RATING: INTERMEDIATE
Size: 65" × 89"
Blocks: 10 (12") Star blocks

MATERIALS

Block print including 10 blocks (or enough to cut 10 (7¾") squares)
1 yard gold print for blocks
¾ yard green print for blocks
1⅛ yards light blue print for blocks
1 yard medium blue print for blocks
½ yard dark blue print for inner border
1⅛ yards black print #1 for blocks
1 yard black print #2 for blocks
2 yards black print #3 for outer border
¾ yard navy print for binding
7¾" square template plastic
Paper for foundations
5½ yards backing fabric
Twin-size quilt batting

NOTE: Fabrics in the quilt shown are from the Space: The New Frontier collection by Benartex.

Cutting

Measurements include ¼" seam allowances. Border strips are exact length needed. You may want to make them longer to allow for piecing variations. For instructions on paper foundation piecing, see *Sew Easy: Paper Foundation Piecing* on page 157.

NOTE: D and E rectangles are cut over-sized for foundation piecing.

From block print, cut:
• 14 (7¾") A squares, centering design on each. Place plastic template square atop fabric; draw around template. Cut on line.

From gold print, cut:
• 9 (2⅞"-wide) strips. From strips, cut 16 (2⅞" × 12½") C rectangles and 16 (2⅞" × 7¾") B rectangles.

From green print, cut:
• 7 (2⅞"-wide) strips. From strips, cut 12 (2⅞" × 12½") C rectangles and 12 (2⅞" × 7¾") B rectangles.

From light blue print, cut:
• 10 (3½"-wide) strips. From strips, cut 40 (3½" × 10") D rectangles.

From medium blue print, cut:
• 8 (3¾"-wide) strips. From strips, cut 40 (3¾" × 8") E rectangles.

From dark blue print, cut:
• 7 (1½"-wide) strips. Piece strips to make 2 (1½" × 72½") side inner borders and 2 (1½" × 50½") top and bottom inner borders.

From black print #1, cut:
• 10 (3½"-wide) strips. From strips, cut 40 (3½" × 10") D rectangles.

From black print #2, cut:
• 8 (3¾"-wide) strips. From strips, cut 40 (3¾" × 8") E rectangles.

From black print #3, cut:
• 8 (8"-wide) strips. Piece strips to make 2 (8" × 74½") side outer borders and 2 (8" × 65½") top and bottom outer borders.

From navy print, cut:
• 9 (2¼"-wide) strips for binding.

Block Assembly

1. Trace or photocopy 40 block segment foundations from the pattern on page 156.

2. Foundation piece block segments in numerical order using light blue print and black print #1 D rectangles, and medium blue print and black print #2 E rectangles *(Block Segment Diagram).* Make 40 Block Segments.

Block Segment Diagram

3. Lay out 4 Block Segments as shown in *Star Block Assembly Diagram.* Join segments into rows; join rows to complete 1 Star block *(Star Block Diagram).* Make 10 Star blocks.

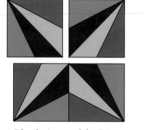

Star Block Assembly Diagram

Star Block Diagram

4. Lay out 1 block print A square, 2 gold print B rectangles, and 2 gold print C rectangles as shown in *Framed Block Assembly Diagram.* Join to complete 1 Framed block *(Framed Block Diagrams).* Make 8 gold Framed blocks.

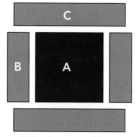

Framed Block Assembly Diagram

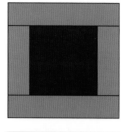

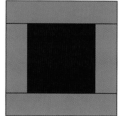

Framed Block Diagrams

5. In the same manner, make 6 green Framed blocks using remaining block print A squares and green print B and C rectangles.

Quilt Assembly

1. Lay out blocks as shown in *Quilt Top Assembly Diagram.* Join into rows; join rows to complete quilt center.

2. Add dark blue print side inner borders to quilt center. Add top and bottom inner borders to quilt.

3. Repeat for black print #3 outer borders.

Finishing

1. Divide backing into 2 (2¾-yard) lengths. Cut 1 piece in half lengthwise to make 2 narrow panels. Join 1 narrow panel to each side of wider panel; press seam allowances toward narrow panels.

2. Layer backing, batting, and quilt top; baste. Quilt as desired. Quilt shown was quilted with an allover design of stars and loops *(Quilting Diagram).*

3. Join 2¼"-wide navy print strips into 1 continuous piece for straight-grain French-fold binding. Add binding to quilt.

Quilting Diagram

TRIED & TRUE

We made a girly version with fabrics from the House collection by Annette Tatum for Free Spirit.

Quilt Top Assembly Diagram

DESIGNER

Debby Kratovil is a prolific quilter, designer, and illustrator. She is a popular teacher both locally and nationally, and loves being in the classroom with motivated quilting students. Debby lives in Virginia with her husband, Phil, and dog, Belle. She has three grown daughters.

Contact her at:

www.quilterbydesign.com ✳

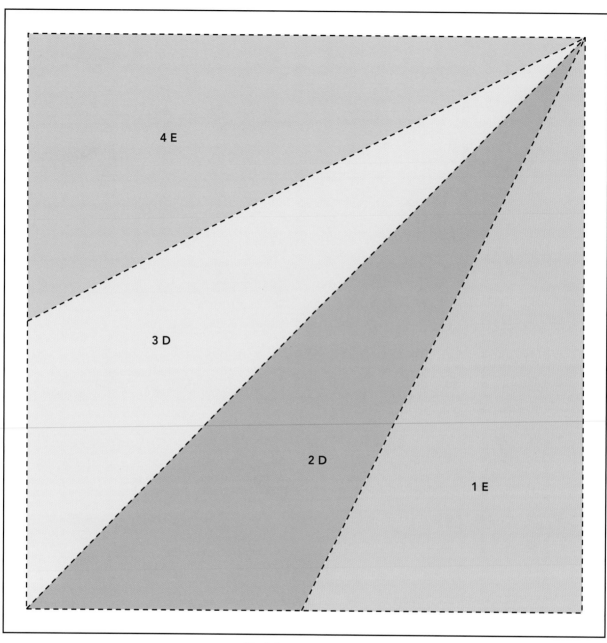

Block Segment Pattern

Paper Foundation Piecing

Paper foundation piecing is ideal for designs with odd angles and sizes of pieces.
Use this method for the Star blocks in *Blast Off* on page 152.

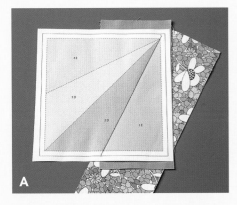

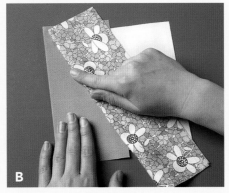

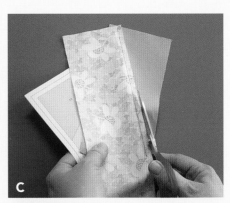

1. Using ruler and pencil, trace all lines and outer edge of foundation pattern onto tracing paper. Number pieces to indicate the stitching order.

> ## Sew Smart™
> Save time by making photocopies on special foundation papers. Check photocopied patterns to be sure they are correct size. (Some copiers may distort copy size.)
> —Liz

2. Using fabric pieces that are larger than the numbered areas, place fabrics for #1 and #2 right sides together. Position paper pattern atop fabrics with printed side of paper facing you. Make sure the fabric for #1 is under that area and that edges of fabrics extend ¼" beyond stitching line between the two sections.

3. Using a short machine stitch so papers will tear off easily later, stitch on line between the two areas, extending stitching into seam allowances at ends of seams (*Photo A*).

4. Open out pieces and press or finger press the seam (*Photo B*). The right sides of the fabric pieces will be facing out on the back side of the paper pattern.

5. Flip the work over and fold back paper pattern on stitched line. Trim seam allowance to ¼", being careful not to cut paper pattern (*Photo C*).

6. Continue to add pieces in numerical order until pattern is covered. Use rotary cutter and ruler to trim excess paper and fabric along outer pattern lines (*Photo D*).

7. Carefully tear off foundation paper after blocks are joined.

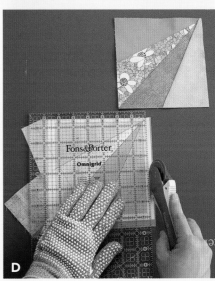

Overnight Bag

Big enough to hold the essentials for an overnight stay, but not too big for a kid to carry easily, this bag is a great gift for an on-the-go youngster.

PROJECT RATING: EASY
Size: 11" × 15"

MATERIALS

½ yard prequilted fabric
3 yards of (¼"-diameter) cord (cut into 2 pieces)
6" of (1"-wide) nylon strap (cut into 2 pieces)

Cutting

Measurements include ½" seam allowances. Zigzag or serge close to edges of cut pieces to prevent seam allowances from fraying as you handle fabrics. Reinforce all seams by stitching a second time, ⅛" from first seam.
From prequilted fabric, cut:
• 2 (12½" × 16½") rectangles.

Assembly

1. Along top edge of 1 bag rectangle, press under 1". Stitch close to raw edge to form casing for cord. Repeat for other bag rectangle.
2. Fold nylon strap pieces in half, aligning raw edges.

3. Pin straps on right side of 1 bag rectangle, about 1" from bottom edge as shown in *Assembly Diagram*. Machine baste in place.

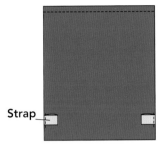

Strap

Assembly Diagram

4. With right sides facing, join bag rectangles on sides and bottom, including ends of strap in seam. Stop at bottom of casing; backstitch to reinforce.

5. Turn bag right side out.

6. Working from left to right, insert 1 cord piece through casing on front; bring same end of cord through casing on back from right to left. Both ends of cord will come out of casings on left side of bag and will form a loop on right side at top of bag. Thread 1 end of cord through cord holder strap on left side of bag and tie ends together *(Cord Diagram)*. Repeat for other cord, bring both ends out on right side, creating a loop on left side. Thread 1 end of cord through cord holder on right side of bag and tie ends together. Adjust cords so tied ends are inside loops.

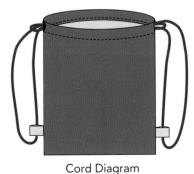

Cord Diagram

Delight a budding ballerina by making her a special bag for her dancing shoes.

TRIED & TRUE

If you can't find prequilted fabric to make the bag, make your own. We used a half yard each of two prints and quilted them, using low-loft polyester batting. The fabric in our version is from Timeless Treasures. ✳

T-shirt Quilts

Making T-shirt quilts is a great way to preserve memories of special places and events. Use tips from designers Colette Cogley and Judy Robey to create a treasured quilt.

PROJECT RATING: EASY

MATERIALS

Cotton T-shirts
Optional: Fabric for sashing and
    binding
Lightweight fusible interfacing
    (approximately 8 yards for a
    twin-size quilt)
Large ruled square
Fabric for backing and binding
Batting

Instructions

1. Collect and launder T-shirts. Using scissors, cut up each side of shirt. Cut off sleeves and neck ribbing *(Photo A)*. Discard ribbing and other pieces that don't contain images or writing.

Photo A

2. Measure logo area of each shirt. Cut a piece of lightweight fusible interfacing at least 1" larger than desired block size. Following manufacturer's instructions, fuse interfacing to wrong side of T-shirt logo area, centering interfacing over design *(Photo B)*.

Photo B

3. Place large ruled square over design area, centering design within desired block size. Use ruled square and rotary cutter to trim interfaced block to desired finished size plus ½" for seam allowances *(Photo C)*.

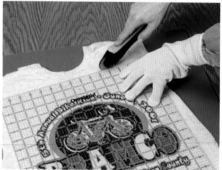

Photo C

4. Repeat for remaining shirts.

5. Lay out blocks and optional sashing. Join blocks to form rows; join rows.

6. Add borders if desired.

7. Layer backing, batting, and quilt top; baste. Quilt as desired. Quilts shown were machine quilted.

8. From binding fabric, make binding and add to quilt.

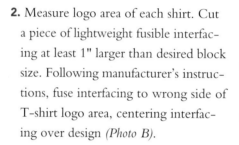

QUILT BY **Colette Cogley of Quiltology**.

MACHINE QUILTED BY **Sally Evanshank**.

Sew **Smart**™
Colette Cogley's Tips for T-Shirt Quilts

1. Create vertical rows of shirts with a common width measurement. Keep in mind children's and small adult-size shirts will be narrower than large adult-size shirts. Keep like widths in the same row.

2. Fuse interfacing to the wrong side of shirts before you cut.

3. Cut common width first for each row, and then cut the height of each shirt. Join into rows, adjusting rows to the same length.

4. Piece squares and rectangles of assorted fabrics for sashing and borders. I like to use solid colors for a contemporary look. Use colors from a school or sports team to add sentimental value.

Contact: Quiltology—the urban quilt space • 1221 W Diversey Pkwy • Chicago, IL 60614 • www.quiltology.com ✳

Sew Smart™

Judy Robey's Tips for T-Shirt Quilts

1. If the shirts in your collection have logos all nearly the same size, choose a block size, and think about making a quilt with same-size blocks separated by sashing.

2. If the T-shirt logo sizes vary widely, make blocks of various sizes, rounding off finished sizes to the nearest even inch. On graph paper, draw a layout for arranging and joining blocks. You may need some filler pieces. Remember to add seam allowances when preparing shirts.

3. For T-shirt quilts you make from your child's school events, choose fabrics in school colors for sashing, binding, and backing.

4. If you own a serger, you might want to use it to join your interfaced blocks.

Mitered Borders

The subtle seam of a mitered corner creates the illusion of a continuous line around the quilt. Mitered corners are ideal for striped fabric borders or multiple plain borders. See *Baby Barnyard* on page 138 and *Rootin' Tootin' Cowboy* on page 142.

1. Referring to *Measuring Quilt Center Diagram*, measure your quilt length through the middle of the quilt rather than along the edges. In the same manner, measure quilt width. Add to your measurements twice the planned width of the border plus 2". Trim borders to these measurements.

Measuring Quilt Center Diagram

2. On wrong side of quilt top, mark ¼" seam allowances at each corner.

3. Fold quilt top in half and place a pin at the center of the quilt side. Fold border in half and mark center with pin.

4. With right sides facing and raw edges aligned, match center pins on the border and the quilt. Working from the center out, pin the border to the quilt, right sides facing. The border will extend beyond the quilt edges. Do not trim the border.

5. Sew the border to the quilt. Start and stop stitching ¼" from the corner of the quilt top, backstitching at each end. Press the seam allowance toward the border. Add the remaining borders in the same manner.

6. With right sides facing, fold the quilt diagonally as shown in *Mitering Diagram 1*, aligning the raw edges of the adjacent borders. Pin securely.

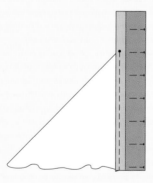

Mitering Diagram 1

7. Align a ruler along the diagonal fold, as shown in *Mitering Diagram 2*. Holding the ruler firmly, mark a line from the end of the border seam to the raw edge.

8. Start machine-stitching at the beginning of the marked line, backstitch, and then stitch on the line out to the raw edge.

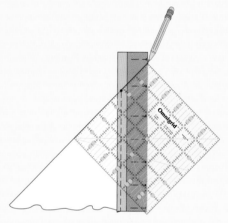

Mitering Diagram 2

9. Unfold the quilt to be sure that the corner lies flat (*Mitered Borders Diagram*). Correct the stitching if necessary. Trim the seam allowance to ¼".

Mitered Borders Diagram

10. Miter the remaining corners. Press the corner seams open.

General Instructions

Basic Supplies

You'll need a **sewing machine (A)** in good working order to construct patchwork blocks, join blocks together, add borders, and machine quilt. We encourage you to purchase a machine from a local dealer, who can help you with service in the future, rather than from a discount store. Another option may be to borrow a machine from a friend or family member. If the machine has not been used in a while, have it serviced by a local dealer to make sure it is in good working order. If you need an extension cord, one with a surge protector is a good idea.

A **rotary cutting mat (B)** is essential for accurate and safe rotary cutting. Purchase one that is no smaller than 18" × 24".

Rotary cutting mats are made of "self-healing" material that can be used over and over.

A **rotary cutter (C)** is a cutting tool that looks like a pizza cutter, and has a very sharp blade. We recommend starting with a standard size 45mm rotary cutter. Always lock or close your cutter when it is not in use, and keep it out of the reach of children.

A **safety glove** (also known as a *Klutz Glove*) **(D)** is also recommended. Wear your safety glove on the hand that is holding the ruler in place. Because it is made of cut-resistant material, the safety glove protects your non-cutting hand from accidents that can occur if your cutting hand slips while cutting.

An acrylic **ruler (E)** is used in combination with your cutting mat and rotary cutter. We recommend the Fons & Porter

8" × 14" ruler, but a 6" × 12" ruler is another good option. You'll need a ruler with inch, quarter-inch, and eighth-inch markings that show clearly for ease of measuring. Choose a ruler with 45-degree-angle, 30-degree-angle, and 60-degree-angle lines marked on it as well.

Since you will be using 100% cotton fabric for your quilts, use **cotton or cotton-covered polyester thread (F)** for piecing and quilting. Avoid 100% polyester thread, as it tends to snarl.

Keep a pair of small **scissors (G)** near your sewing machine for cutting threads.

Thin, good quality **straight pins (H)** are preferred by quilters. The pins included with pincushions are normally too thick to use for piecing, so discard them. Purchase a box of nickel-plated brass **safety pins** size #1 **(I)** to use for pin-basting the layers of your quilt together for machine quilting.

Invest in a 120"-long dressmaker's **measuring tape (J)**. This will come in handy when making borders for your quilt.

A 0.7–0.9mm mechanical **pencil (K)** works well for marking on your fabric.

Invest in a quality sharp **seam ripper (L)**. Every quilter gets well-acquainted with her seam ripper!

Set up an **ironing board (M)** and **iron (N)** in your sewing area. Pressing yardage before cutting, and pressing patchwork seams as you go are both essential for quality quiltmaking. Select an iron that has steam capability.

Masking **tape (O)** or painter's tape works well to mark your sewing machine so you can sew an accurate ¼" seam. You will also use tape to hold your backing fabric taut as you prepare your quilt sandwich for machine quilting.

The most exciting item that you will need for quilting is **fabric (P)**. Quilters generally prefer 100% cotton fabrics for their quilts. This fabric is woven from cotton threads, and has a lengthwise and a crosswise grain. The term "bias" is used to describe the diagonal grain of the fabric. If you make a 45-degree angle cut through a square of cotton fabric, the cut edges will be bias edges, which are quite stretchy. As you learn more quiltmaking techniques, you'll learn how bias can work to your advantage or disadvantage.

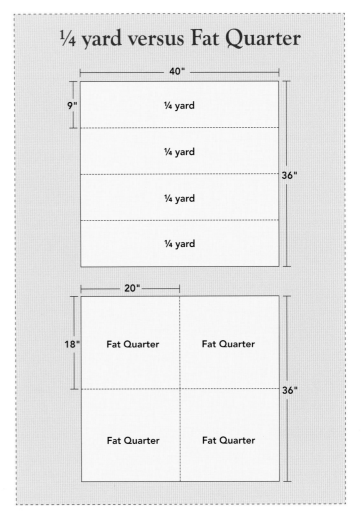

¼ yard versus Fat Quarter

Fabric is sold by the yard at quilt shops and fabric stores. Quilting fabric is generally about 40"–44" wide, so a yard is about 40" wide by 36" long. As you collect fabrics to build your own personal stash, you will buy yards, half yards (about 18" × 40"), quarter yards (about 9" × 40"), as well as other lengths.

Many quilt shops sell "fat quarters," a special cut favored by quilters. A fat quarter is created by cutting a half yard down the fold line into two 18" × 20" pieces (fat quarters) that are sold separately. Quilters like the nearly square shape of the fat quarter because it is more useful than the narrow regular quarter yard cut.

Batting (Q) is the filler between quilt top and backing that makes your quilt a quilt. It can be cotton, polyester, cotton-polyester blend, wool, silk, or other natural materials, such as bamboo or corn. Make sure the batting you buy is at least six inches wider and six inches longer than your quilt top.

Accurate Cutting

Measuring and cutting accuracy are important for successful quilting. Measure at least twice, and cut once!

Cut strips across the fabric width unless directed otherwise.

Cutting for patchwork usually begins with cutting strips, which are then cut into smaller pieces. First, cut straight strips from a fat quarter:

1. Fold fat quarter in half with selvage edge at the top (*Photo A*).

2. Straighten edge of fabric by placing ruler atop fabric, aligning one of the lines on ruler with selvage edge of fabric (*Photo B*). Cut along right edge of ruler.

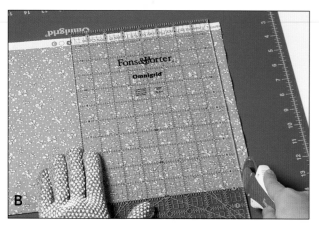

3. Rotate fabric, and use ruler to measure from cut edge to desired strip width (*Photo C*). Measurements in instructions include ¼" seam allowances.

4. After cutting the required number of strips, cut strips into squares or rectangles as needed.

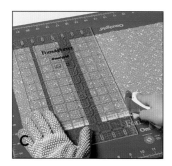

Setting up Your Sewing Machine

Sew Accurate ¼" Seams

Standard seam width for patchwork and quiltmaking is ¼". Some machines come with a patchwork presser foot, also known as a quarter-inch foot. If your machine doesn't have a quarter-inch foot, you may be able to purchase one from a dealer. Or, you can create a quarter-inch seam guide on your machine using masking tape or painter's tape.

Place an acrylic ruler on your sewing machine bed under the presser foot. Slowly turn handwheel until the tip of the needle barely rests atop the ruler's quarter-inch mark (*Photo A*). Make sure the lines on the ruler are parallel to the lines on the machine throat plate. Place tape on the machine bed along edge of ruler (*Photo B*).

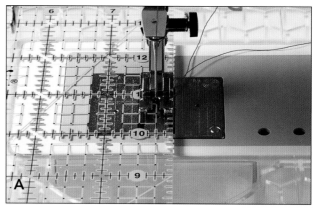

Take a Simple Seam Test

Seam accuracy is critical to machine piecing, so take this simple test once you have your quarter-inch presser foot on your machine or have created a tape guide.

Place 2 (2½") squares right sides together, and sew with a scant ¼" seam. Open squares and finger press seam. To finger press, with right sides facing you, press the seam to one side with your fingernail. Measure across pieces, raw edge to raw edge (*Photo C*). If they measure 4½", you have passed the test! Repeat the test as needed to make sure you can confidently sew a perfect ¼" seam.

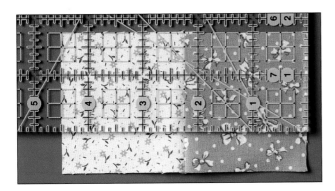

Sewing Comfortably

Other elements that promote pleasant sewing are good lighting, a comfortable chair, background music—and chocolate! Good lighting promotes accurate sewing. The better you can see what you are working on, the better your results. A comfortable chair enables you to sew for longer periods of time. An office chair with a good back rest and adjustable height works well. Music helps keep you relaxed. Chocolate is, for many quilters, simply a necessity.

Tips for Patchwork and Pressing

As you sew more patchwork, you'll develop your own shortcuts and favorite methods. Here are a few favored by many quilters:

- As you join patchwork units to form rows, and join rows to form blocks, press seams in opposite directions from row to row whenever possible (*Photo A*). By pressing seams one direction in the first row and the opposite direction in the next row, you will often create seam allowances that abut when rows are joined (*Photo B*). Abutting or nesting seams are ideal for forming perfectly matched corners on the right side of your quilt blocks and quilt top. Such pressing is not always possible, so don't worry if you end up with seam allowances facing the same direction as you join units.

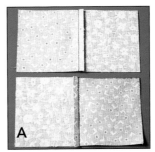 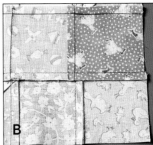

- Sew on and off a small, folded fabric square to prevent bobbin thread from bunching at throat plate (*Photo C*). You'll also save thread, which means fewer stops to wind bobbins, and fewer hanging threads to be snipped. Repeated use of the small piece of fabric gives it lots of thread "legs," so some quilters call it a spider.

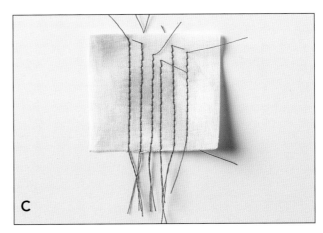

● Chain piece patchwork to reduce the amount of thread you use, and minimize the number and length of threads you need to trim from patchwork. Without cutting threads at the end of a seam, take 3–4 stitches without any fabric under the needle, creating a short thread chain approximately ⅛" long (*Photo D*). Repeat until you have a long line of pieces. Remove chain from machine, clip threads between units, and press seams.

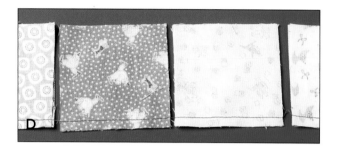

● Trim off tiny triangle tips (sometimes called dog ears) created when making triangle-square units (*Photo E*). Trimming triangles reduces bulk and makes patchwork units and blocks lie flatter. Though no one will see the back of your quilt top once it's quilted, a neat back free of dangling threads and patchwork points is the mark of a good quilter. Also, a smooth, flat quilt top is easier to quilt, whether by hand or machine.

● Careful pressing will make your patchwork neat and crisp, and will help make your finished quilt top lie flat. Ironing and pressing are two different skills. Iron fabric to remove wrinkles using a back and forth, smoothing motion. Press patchwork and quilt blocks by raising and gently lowering the iron atop your work. After sewing a patchwork unit, first press the seam with the unit closed, pressing to set, or embed, the stitching. Setting the seam this way will help produce straight, crisp seams. Open the unit and press on the right side with the seam toward the darkest fabric,

being careful to not form a pleat in your seam, and carefully pressing the patchwork flat.

● Many quilters use finger pressing to open and flatten seams of small units before pressing with an iron. To finger press, open patchwork unit with right side of fabric facing you. Run your fingernail firmly along seam, making sure unit is fully open with no pleat.

● Careful use of steam in your iron will make seams and blocks crisp and flat (*Photo F*). Aggressive ironing can stretch blocks out of shape, and is a common pitfall for new quilters.

Adding Borders

Follow these simple instructions to make borders that fit perfectly on your quilt.

1. Find the length of your quilt by measuring through the quilt center, not along the edges, since the edges may have stretched. Take 3 measurements and average them to determine the length to cut your side borders (*Diagram A*). Cut 2 side borders this length.

2. Fold border strips in half to find center. Pinch to create crease mark or place a pin at center. Fold quilt top in half crosswise to find center of side. Attach side borders to quilt center by pinning them at the ends and the center, and easing in any fullness. If quilt edge is a bit longer than border, pin and sew with border on top; if border is

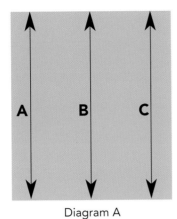

Diagram A

A _____

B _____

C _____

TOTAL _____

÷3

_____

AVERAGE
LENGTH _____

HELPFUL TIP
Use the following decimal conversions to calculate
your quilt's measurements:

$\frac{1}{8}$" = .125	$\frac{5}{8}$" = .625
$\frac{1}{4}$" = .25	$\frac{3}{4}$" = .75
$\frac{3}{8}$" = .375	$\frac{7}{8}$" = .875
$\frac{1}{2}$" = .5	

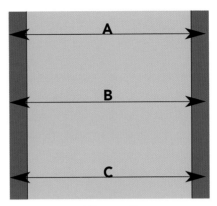

Diagram B

4. Mark centers of borders and top and bottom edges
of quilt top. Attach top and bottom borders to quilt,
pinnning at ends and center, and easing in any fullness
(*Diagram C*). Press seams toward borders.

Diagram C

5. Gently steam press entire quilt top on one side and then
the other. When pressing on wrong side, trim off any
loose threads.

---

slightly longer than quilt top, pin and sew with border on
the bottom. Machine feed dogs will ease in the fullness of
the longer piece. Press seams toward borders.

3. Find the width of your quilt by measuring across the
quilt and side borders (*Diagram B*). Take 3 measurements
and average them to determine the length to cut your
top and bottom borders. Cut 2 borders this length.

Joining Border Strips

Not all quilts have borders, but they are a nice complement to a quilt top. If your border is longer than 40", you will need to join 2 or more strips to make a border the required length. You can join border strips with either a straight seam parallel to the ends of the strips (*Photo A*), or with a diagonal seam. For the diagonal seam method, place one border strip perpendicular to another strip, rights sides facing (*Photo B*). Stitch diagonally across strips as shown. Trim seam allowance to ¼". Press seam open (*Photo C*).

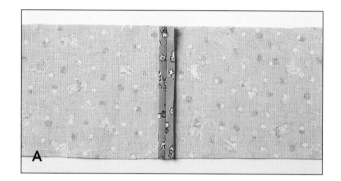

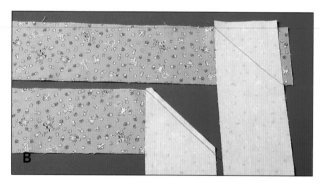

Quilting Your Quilt

Quilters today joke that there are three ways to quilt a quilt—by hand, by machine, or by check. Some enjoy making quilt tops so much, they prefer to hire a professional machine quilter to finish their work. The Split Nine Patch baby quilt shown above has simple machine quilting that you can do yourself.

Decide what color thread will look best on your quilt top before choosing your backing fabric. A thread color that will blend in with the quilt top is a good choice for beginners. Choose backing fabric that will blend with your thread as well. A print fabric is a good choice for hiding less-than-perfect machine quilting. The backing fabric must be at least 3"–4" larger than your quilt top on all 4 sides. For example: if your quilt top measures 44" × 44", your backing needs to be at least 50" × 50". If your quilt top is 80" × 96", then your backing fabric needs to be at least 86" × 102".

For quilt tops 36" wide or less, use a single width of fabric for the backing. Buy enough length to allow adequate margin at quilt edges, as noted above. When your quilt is wider than 36", one option is to use 60"-, 90"-, or 108"-wide fabric for the quilt backing. Because fabric selection is limited for wide fabrics, quilters generally piece the quilt backing from 44/45"-wide fabric. Plan on 40"–42" of usable fabric width when estimating how much fabric to purchase. Plan your piecing strategy to avoid having a seam along the veritcal or horizontal center of the quilt.

For a quilt 37"–60" wide, a backing with horizontal seams is usually the most economical use of fabric. For example, for a quilt 50" × 70", vertical seams would require 152", or 4¼ yards, of 44/45"-wide fabric (76" + 76" = 152"). Horizontal seams would require 112", or 3¼ yards (56" + 56" = 112").

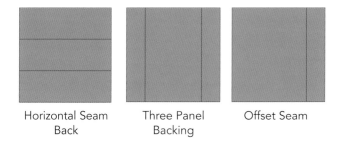

Horizontal Seam Back   Three Panel Backing   Offset Seam

For a quilt 61"–80" wide, most quilters piece a three-panel backing, with vertical seams, from two lengths of fabric. Cut one of the pieces in half lengthwise, and sew the halves to opposite sides of the wider panel. Press the seams away from the center panel.

For a quilt 81"–120" wide, you will need three lengths of fabric, plus extra margin. For example, for a quilt 108" × 108", purchase at least 342", or 9½ yards, of 44/45"-wide fabric (114" + 114" + 114" = 342").

For a three-panel backing, pin the selvage edge of the center panel to the selvage edge of the side panel, with edges aligned and right sides facing. Machine stitch with a ½" seam. Trim seam allowances to ¼", trimming off the selvages from both panels at once. Press the seam away from the center of the quilt. Repeat on other side of center panel.

For a two-panel backing, join panels in the same manner as above, and press the seam to one side.

Create a "quilt sandwich" by layering your backing, batting, and quilt top. Find the crosswise center of the backing fabric by folding it in half. Mark with a pin on each side. Lay backing down on a table or floor, wrong side up. Tape corners and edges of backing to the surface with masking or painter's tape so that backing is taut (*Photo A*).

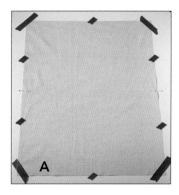

Fold batting in half crosswise and position it atop backing fabric, centering folded edge at center of backing (*Photo B*). Unfold batting and smooth it out atop backing (*Photo C*).

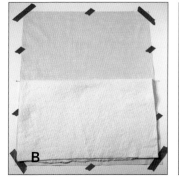
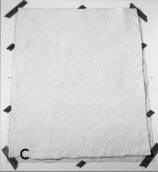

In the same manner, fold the quilt top in half crosswise and center it atop backing and batting (*Photo D*). Unfold top and smooth it out atop batting (*Photo E*).

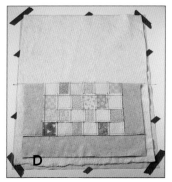

Use safety pins to pin baste the layers (*Photo F*). Pins should be about a fist width apart. A special tool, called a Kwik Klip, or a grapefruit spoon makes closing the pins easier. As you slide a pin through all three layers, slide the point of the pin into one of the tool's grooves. Push on the tool to help close the pin.

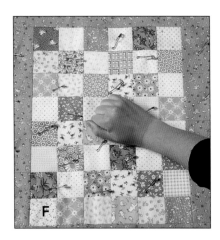

For straight line quilting, install an even feed or walking foot on your machine. This presser foot helps all three layers of your quilt move through the machine evenly without bunching.

Walking Foot

Stitching "in the ditch"

An easy way to quilt your first quilt is to stitch "in the ditch" along seam lines. No marking is needed for this type of quilting.

Binding Your Quilt

Preparing Binding

Strips for quilt binding may be cut either on the straight of grain or on the bias. For the quilts in this booklet, cut strips on the straight of grain.

1. Measure the perimeter of your quilt and add approximately 24" to allow for mitered corners and finished ends.

2. Cut the number of strips necessary to achieve desired length. We like to cut binding strips 2¼" wide.

3. Join your strips with diagonal seams into 1 continuous piece (*Photo A*). Press the seams open. (See page 170 for instructions for the diagonal seams method of joining strips.)

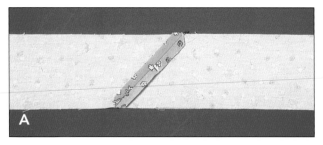

4. Press your binding in half lengthwise, with wrong sides facing, to make French-fold binding (*Photo B*).

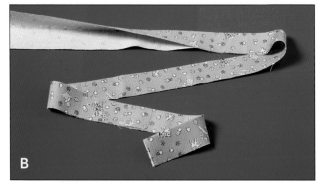

Attaching Binding

Attach the binding to your quilt using an even-feed or walking foot. This prevents puckering when sewing through the three layers.

1. Choose beginning point along one side of quilt. Do not start at a corner. Match the two raw edges of the binding strip to the raw edge of the quilt top. The folded edge

will be free and to left of seam line (*Photo C*). Leave 12"
or longer tail of binding strip dangling free from beginning point. Stitch, using ¼" seam, through all layers.

Bring binding straight down in line with next edge to be
sewn, leaving top fold even with raw edge of previously
sewn side (*Photo F*). Begin stitching at top edge, sewing
through all layers (*Photo G*).

2. For mitered corners, stop stitching ¼" from corner;
    backstitch, and remove quilt from sewing machine
    (*Photo D*). Place a pin ¼" from corner to mark where
    you will stop stitching.

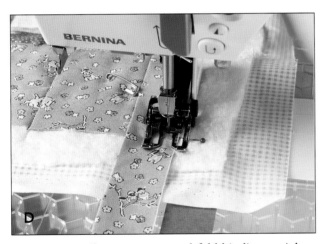

Rotate quilt quarter turn and fold binding straight up,
away from corner, forming 45-degree-angle fold (*Photo E*).

3. To finish binding, stop stitching about 8" away from
    starting point, leaving about a 12" tail at end (*Photo
    H*). Bring beginning and end of binding to center of
    8" opening and fold each back, leaving about ¼" space

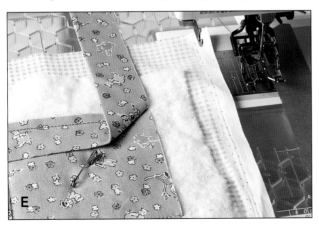

between the two folds of binding (*Photo I*). (Allowing this ¼" extra space is critical, as binding tends to stretch when it is stitched to the quilt. If the folded ends meet at this point, your binding will be too long for the space after the ends are joined.) Crease folds of binding with your fingernail.

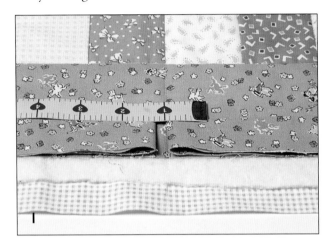

4. Open out each edge of binding and draw line across wrong side of binding on creased fold line, as shown in *Photo J*. Draw line along lengthwise fold of binding at same spot to create an X (*Photo K*).

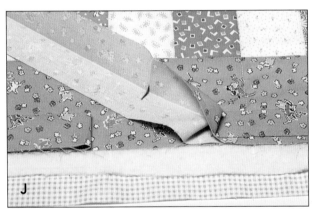

5. With edge of ruler at marked X, line up 45-degree-angle marking on ruler with one long side of binding (*Photo L*). Draw diagonal line across binding as shown in *Photo M*.

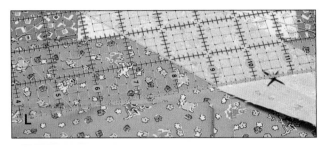

Repeat for other end of binding. Lines must angle in same direction (*Photo N*).

6. Pin binding ends together with right sides facing, pin-matching diagonal lines as shown in *Photo O*. Binding ends will be at right angles to each other. Machine-stitch along diagonal line, removing pins as you stitch (*Photo P*).

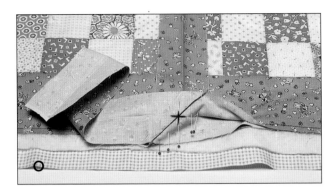

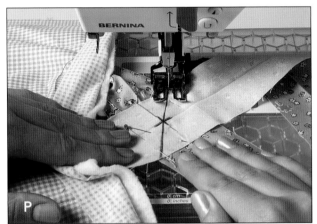

7. Lay binding against quilt to double-check that it is correct length (*Photo Q*). Trim ends of binding ¼" from diagonal seam (*Photo R*).

8. Finger press diagonal seam open (*Photo S*). Fold binding in half and finish stitching binding to quilt (*Photo T*).

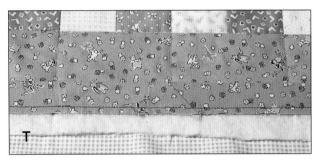

Hand Stitching Binding to Quilt Back

1. Trim any excess batting and quilt back with scissors or a rotary cutter (*Photo A*). Leave enough batting (about ⅛" beyond quilt top) to fill binding uniformly when it is turned to quilt back.

2. Bring folded edge of binding to quilt back so that it covers machine stitching. Blindstitch folded edge to quilt backing, using a few pins just ahead of stitching to hold binding in place (*Photo B*).

3. Continue stitching to corner. Fold unstitched binding from next side under, forming a 45-degree angle and a mitered corner. Stitch mitered folds on both front and back (*Photo C*).

Finishing Touches

● **Label your quilt so the recipient and future generations know who made it.** To make a label, use a fabric marking pen to write the details on a small piece of solid color fabric (*Photo A*). To make writing easier, put pieces of masking tape on the wrong side. Remove tape after writing. Use your iron to turn under ¼" on each edge, then stitch the label to the back of your quilt using a blindstitch, taking care not to sew through to quilt top.

● **Take a photo of your quilt.** Keep your photos in an album or journal along with notes, fabric swatches, and other information about the quilts.

● **If your quilt is a gift, include care instructions.** Some quilt shops carry pre-printed care labels you can sew onto the quilt (*Photo B*). Or, make a care label using the method described above.

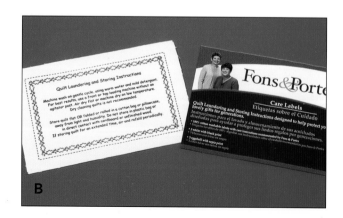